They'll Fight Over It When You're Dead

They'll Fight Over It When You're Dead

The True Story of How I Survived
Terrorists, Morons and an Assassin to
Build One of the Coolest
Leather Companies in the World

DAVE MUNSON

Forefront
BOOKS

They'll Fight Over It When You're Dead: The True Story of How I Survived Terrorists, Morons and an Assassin to Build One of the Coolest Leather Companies in the World
Copyright © 2025 by Dave Munson

All rights reserved. No part of this publication may be reproduced, stored in a retrieval system, or transmitted in any form by any means, electronic, mechanical, photocopy, recording, or otherwise, without the prior permission of the publisher, except as provided by USA copyright law.

No patent liability is assumed with respect to the use of the information contained herein. Although every precaution has been taken in the preparation of this book, the publisher and author assume no responsibility for errors or omissions. Neither is any liability assumed for damages resulting from the use of the information contained herein.

Most names and some identifying details have been changed, whether or not so noted in the text.

Scripture quotations marked BSB are taken from the Holy Bible, Berean Standard Bible, BSB is produced in cooperation with Bible Hub, Discovery Bible, OpenBible.com, and the Berean Bible Translation Committee. Public domain.

Published by Forefront Books, Nashville, Tennessee.
Distributed by Simon & Schuster.

Library of Congress Control Number: 2025906483

Print ISBN: 978-1-63763-420-2
E-book ISBN: 978-1-63763-421-9

Cover Design by Michelle Manley
Interior Design by Interior Design by PerfecType, Nashville, TN

Printed in the United States of America

25 26 27 28 29 30 LSC 10 9 8 7 6 5 4 3 2 1

CONTENTS

Introduction **11**

• **ONE** • Tanned and Toughened **17**
• **TWO** • Adios America **27**
• **THREE** • Everybody Wants One **43**
• **FOUR** • To Murder My Assassin **51**
• **FIVE** • Selling Leather the Hard Way **71**
• **SIX** • Family to the Rescue **93**
• **SEVEN** • Life and Death **107**
• **EIGHT** • Handing Over the Reins **117**
• **NINE** • Alive in Africa **127**
• **TEN** • How to Be the Boss **141**
• **ELEVEN** • Independence Day **151**
• **TWELVE** • Tents and Terrorists **157**
• **THIRTEEN** • Toyota Meets Their Match **175**
• **FOURTEEN** • The Life Altering Gift **189**
• **FIFTEEN** • Walking with Kings **209**
• **CONCLUSION** • Saddleback Leather Today **227**

Acknowledgments **229**

To my beautiful wife, Suzette. After being married to you for all of these years, my only regret is that I didn't marry you sooner. Take me out to the ballgame baby and show me the treasure.

It is not the critic who counts; not the man who points out how the strong man stumbles, or where the doer of deeds could have done them better. The credit belongs to the man who is actually in the arena, whose face is marred by dust and sweat and blood; who strives valiantly; who errs, who comes short again and again, because there is no effort without error and shortcoming; but who does actually strive to do the deeds; who knows great enthusiasms, the great devotions; who spends himself in a worthy cause; who at the best knows in the end the triumph of high achievement, and who at the worst, if he fails, at least fails while daring greatly, so that his place shall never be with those cold and timid souls who neither know victory nor defeat.
—Theodore Roosevelt, "The Man in the Arena" (1910)

INTRODUCTION

I shed a lot of blood, sweat and tears trying to get my company, Saddleback Leather, up and going, and it wasn't all mine. This book does not tell a traditional "How I Started" story. I have hit many bumps in the road along the way. A Mexican *federale* was sent to kill me, but I decided to kill him instead. I'm pretty sure I unintentionally worked for the Mexican mafia for a couple of years. For 3 long years, my black Lab, Blue, and I slept on the floor of a $100 a month apartment in the most dangerous city in the world, with no hot water, trying to get this business going.

Blue and I drove at least 100,000 miles all over North America without a radio in a slow and noisy 1971 FJ55 Toyota Land Cruiser that only got about 13 gallons per mile and 20,000 of those miles were driven with white knuckles on bad Mexican roads. I had lots of time to think about things as I drove, because Blue wasn't much of a talker, but he was a good listener, and more than that, a dear and faithful friend (so much so that I immortalized him in the Saddleback Leather logo).

We slept cold and hot and restless hundreds of times in, around or on the rack of the Land Cruiser. I crashed, went homeless, killed, was bribed, bribed, hitchhiked, got robbed, broke down and went sleepless and hungry for weeks at a time. Blue got stolen once, and millions of dollars managed to disappear out of the company a couple of times (How awesome is it that I ever had that much money to lose!) I fought a bull in a Mexican bullfight, and twice I traded Blue's stud fee puppies for tacos so I could eat right. Today, Blue's healthy and fresh blood runs through the veins of many a dog in Mexico and the United States.

The journey has been amazing. While accidentally creating Saddleback Leather, I met amazing people. The most amazing is a fun and sexy woman, Suzette. We met, started kissing and got married. Nine months and 15 minutes later, our sweet little girl named Sela (rhymes with *fella*) was born. And then Suzette bore me a smart and handsome manchild and chess partner named Cross. I was single until I was 35, and my family thought I was being way too picky. My sister, Debbie, told me I really needed to shorten my list because the woman I had there didn't exist. I told her to wait and see. Well, I got everything on the list, when I married Suzette, except that she wasn't 5'8", but I got everything else though. I honestly feel like I won the marriage lottery (most of the time).

Suzette's compassion and love for the fatherless expanded our family to include a good number of Rwandan and Ugandan orphans, whom we proudly call sons. She also initiated a fun English language homeschool at our leather factory in Mexico. There is no one on Earth who brings more light and joy into my life than Suzette.

GOD, LEATHER AND GOOD TIMES

I need to make sure you know something before you keep on reading. A lot of real cool things have happened and are happening while getting this little leather company up and running. Sometimes it may sound like I'm bragging, but I'm just telling the story as it happened. There is nothing inside of us that makes us more special than the next guy. We weren't born superior to anyone, nor have we become that. The only way I can explain how this cool story came together is that God decided it would happen. He chooses ordinary people and uses them to do things that bring people to know Him in a more personal way.

I will take credit for most of the sad, hard and awkward things that have happened while getting Saddleback going though. I've messed up and failed too many times to be able to take credit for anything good that has happened. I want to encourage those who feel down in the dumps and think about quitting, to not quit. Everybody makes mistakes as they try to get things going. You can't have any success without them. But the sooner you get the mistakes out of the way, the sooner the good times will start rolling. It's just the way it is. Go for it and stick with it. Remember, by perseverance, the snails reached the ark.

God does strange things that you'd never expect when you just start. He introduced us to a good number of kings, queens and emperors, and we've even had a few of them come stay in our tents where we live in Texas (Don't feel sorry for us, they're pretty cool tents). I've been interviewed on Fox News, CBS, NPR and other national broadcasts, and our marketing videos have even made it onto national TV.

Our leather bags have appeared in Hollywood movies, and part of this story, and what we do, has been written into many fiction and nonfiction books by authors who are owners of our leather bags. Saddleback Leather even made it into a Tom Clancy novel and two McGraw Hill college marketing textbooks. Toyota recently launched the Limited Edition Tundra, of which I designed the interior of with them, and Rolls Royce put us in their Enthusiast Club's coffee table book because of our love for quality and design. Martin Guitar asked if we could work on a special edition Saddleback Leather guitar with them, and Major League Baseball asked us to not just provide the Official Leather Goods of the World Series Champion Texas Rangers, but asked us to offer our high quality leather goods for the rest of the league's teams too. And in my office hangs a letter from President

George W. Bush complimenting us on the cool Saddleback Leather luggage he owns.

All of these things confirm to us that we're doing something right. It could be the excessive quality built into the designs that people are drawn to, or how we take the time to educate people on what quality is. Maybe it's even our unprofessional and not funny marketing. Whatever the reason, we have treated challenges as stepping stones leading us toward the truly meaningful work we believe God is starting to reveal to us.

We are a people business cleverly disguised as a leather bag company.

WHY I WROTE THIS BOOK

This book tells the story of how I accidentally started what a lot of our customers have called "one of the coolest leather companies in the world," along with the fun and hard times that came with it. As you will see, I didn't develop a business plan until well after I'd started the company. Instead, I just started shipping bags and figured out the boring stuff later.

Right away, I had to get good at listening to those who knew how to do things better than I did. Throughout this book, I'll pass along valuable lessons I learned as I was developing the company just in case you want to avoid some of the hard lessons I had to learn.

As I tell my story, it will become clear that I am a Christian who believes that God plays a rather active role in the world. I'm also the kind of person who speaks directly and plainly, much to the annoyance of some Christians. I'm cool with people who disagree with me, but I ask that you be cool with me back. If you're a delicate and sensitive pussywillow who always gets their feelings hurt or who gets offended for other people when someone shares a thought or opinion that is different from yours, then you might want to stop reading this book right now. Or if you're one of those fakey, judgmental Christians who looks down their superior nose at anyone who doesn't have the same elevated thinking as you, then you might want to put this book down too. Basically, if you're not the kind of person who can eat the fish and spit out the bones, you might find parts of this book tough to swallow. But stick with me. I think you'll appreciate, or at least be entertained by, most of what I have to say.

I'm just going to describe what happened as I created this company, where my mind goes on all sorts of topics and what I personally believe. I'm not saying I'm right and everyone who doesn't believe, think or act exactly like I do is wrong. I'm just telling you what's in my head and heart and what has had significant impact in my own personal life, family and business. You can choose what to do with all of it.

My main hope for the book is that it encourages you to take a risk and try that thing you've been wanting to try or needing to take the next step with. I don't mean you should try things that could cause you serious hurt or financial ruin (though I'm not saying you shouldn't), but rather the things you think a lot about or that give you butterflies. Go for it. You'll live.

I like what Thomas Edison said along the way to creating his lightbulb: "I have not failed. I've just found 10,000 ways that won't work." I found 10,000 ways a business won't work before I found what did. We all have to try things and fail before we succeed. The way you get good at playing guitar is by playing guitar. The way you get good at taking pictures is by taking pictures. Likewise, the way you get good at doing business or traveling or designing or stepping out in faith is by doing it.

And you'll know you're doing the right thing when you start getting criticized for no good reason. It's weird. I've been criticized a thousand times for doing business all wrong. Some criticism was helpful and some I deserved for being dumb, but often it was just from someone all mad that I wasn't "following the rules."

Remember the passage from Theodore Roosevelt's "The Man in the Arena" speech, which I quoted at the start of this book? Roosevelt said, "It is not the critic who counts . . . The credit belongs to the man who is actually in the arena." That quote makes me feel good every time I read it. May that be said of you.

I also hope that some of my experiences might connect with you or your business or your relationships in a way that you will be better off knowing about. Maybe you'll feel my pain and that will be good enough to keep you from going there too. But I learned a lot from wise business coaches, friends, my wise father and good ol' trial and error that I put into practice, and it eventually worked out really, really well.

For example, we aren't a huge company, but I've been told a hundred times that Saddleback Leather has one of the strongest brands in the world. So, I'm going to share with you how I defined the brand in order to help you define your own personal or business brand too. These will help you figure out what you should you do in life, how to force yourself to innovate and how to motivate the people around you to action.

I'm also going to share, specifically and simply, how to come up with an attractive and powerful vision, whether for your family, your business, your ministry or your life that will pull for its own fulfillment. One that people will want to be a part of and help make happen.

Finally, I hope to encourage you to follow my example of sharing with others what you've learned, what matters to you or what has helped you in your own relationships, business or in life. Don't hide it. What you say may not help the first 1000 people who hear you, but maybe it'll help the next one or two. And they'll be thankful you were confident enough to ignore the judgers and speak up.

I wrote this book because we are a people company cleverly disguised as a leather bag business, and may your story be that your marriage, parenting, work, relationship with God or purpose in life is stronger because you read the Saddleback Story.

Tanned and Toughened

It's hard to recognize if you're dumb. You're used to yourself and so you think your dumbness is normal. It's like bad breath. You get used to it, but when you open your mouth, others know it right away. I wasn't super dumb, but I recognized I was pretty slow to organize and articulate my thoughts, and I certainly wasn't disciplined enough to study much on my own. I needed help. So, I paid a lot of money for a university to force me to learn and shape the way my mind works. And that's what happened at Multnomah Bible College in Portland, Oregon.

In June of 1996, I graduated with a Bachelor's degree in Theology with a Minor in Ancient Greek. I thought I was going to be a pastor of a church one day. Those areas of study aren't widely considered useful subjects for starting and running a business, but if I were to go back and tell my 18 year old self that I was going to start this leather business, I wouldn't change my studies at all, though I would have gotten a tutor for Accounting 101. It was the hardest class I ever had, because my mind just didn't go there. I actually got a D minus because

I found something I liked about my teacher and complimented her every single day on it. It's a good thing "D's get degrees."

After graduation, I wasn't sure what I would do next, so I did what I'd done the summer before: take groups into Juarez, Mexico to build homes. We would build a basic 11' x 22' house where a family's old cardboard home had sat before.

After a summer spent building houses, I moved to a cool little town in southern New Mexico called Truth or Consequences, affectionately known as T or C, where my dad was pastoring a church. The town was named after an old TV game show. I figured it was a great place to start up a youth group, since my dad's small church didn't have a youth pastor and my 13 year old little brother, Jonathan, needed one. I had volunteered under a couple of youth pastors for the past seven years, and it seemed like such a fun and easy job. Camping, rolling rocks off cliffs, playing games, skipping rocks, hanging out with kids and pulling fingers was a blast. What was not to love? And it was especially cool because I got to hang out with my little brother and teach him and his friends about life and God.

But there was a problem. A big group of old people at the church said they didn't want youth in the church. They said they were retired and had already done their time dealing with kids, and now just wanted a retired people's church. They said if the church decided to pay me, then they would stop tithing and force my dad out.

So, to get around the problem, I started "volunteering," and they couldn't say a thing about it. On the side, several kind church members, generally the parents with teenagers, chipped in to give me about $300 each month. Since I was living rent free in a little house Mom and Dad owned, it worked out. While I wasn't living high on the hog, those 3 years were some of the best years of my life.

The soft skills I learned being a youth pastor shaped me, and therefore shaped Saddleback Leather into what it is today. I grew up with 3 older sisters, so I got kind of thick skin from them, but all the criticism and attacks I got as a youth pastor from those old goats and the occasional angry parent at the church thickened up my skin even more. Now, as a business owner who's trying to do more than just sell leather bags, I get tons of criticism for everything. One time, someone posted that they hoped that on our next trip to Africa, that our kids would be kidnapped and sold into sex slavery. Let's just chalk that one up to pure evil.

I learned public speaking by preparing and delivering talks every Wednesday night for 3 years to the kids. I had to explain hard to understand subjects in simple and fun ways that they could understand. That was great practice. And now, when I try to explain leather or quality or why you should pay more for something instead of a cheaper alternative, it's easier to get my point across. But looking back, the most important thing I learned during those years was that I was a very prideful man and God was gently resisting me at first, just like He may be resisting you. I always thought pride was just being cocky or bragging a lot, but little did I know it takes a lot of other forms that I didn't know were pride. Now that I'm more aware of them, I'm prideful less often, but it's still a problem.

THE PERFECT COMPANION

While I was having tons of fun working with youth, I realized something was missing from my life. Some roads just aren't meant to be traveled alone. In July of 1997, I was lonely and needed a cheap companion, someone loyal, friendly, forgiving, who loved me unconditionally and who was low maintenance too. Someone who was a good listener, who adored me and who would always stay by my side. In other words, I needed a dog. I don't think there's a single person on the planet who has as many of those qualities as a dog does. If you don't believe me, put your dog and your spouse in the trunk of the car for an hour. When you open the trunk, who do you think will still be happy to see you?

I had always wanted a dog, but not just any dog. I wanted a black Labrador retriever. I told my friend Nancy about that lifelong dream and not long after, her sister, Virginia, approached me after church and said, "Hey, Dave, I heard you want to own a black Lab one day?" I smiled and told her she'd heard right. She went on to tell me she was a Labrador breeder and that her bitch had just had puppies. And when the puppies were 6 weeks old, she would let me pick out one of the 3 black males for free.

I was so excited, I almost cried when the day finally arrived. I drove to Virginia's house, got down on my hands and knees and played with all 3 of them. But how was I to choose? Then I had an idea that may just give me a sign. I went out to my 1977 VW Westfalia Bus and got my guitar, then went back inside and lined up the 3 puppies and strummed a few chords. One of the puppies just lay there with his chin on the ground, one got scared and ran under the chair and one started wagging his tail. The results were telling, but I wanted to make sure. So, we lined them up again and I strummed the guitar. Just as I had hoped, the same thing happened. One lay there, one ran away and one wagged his tail.

As I started walking toward the door with my new puppy, Virginia's little boy commented, "Oh, you picked the puppy that wags his tail all the time." And he never stopped. He'd wag his tail while he was eating, while he had his chin on my shoulder looking down the highway with me or even when I would throw a rock into a lake for him to fetch. He would dive underwater and sometimes his tail would be the only thing sticking out of the water, and it was wagging.

As soon as I got into the bus with my new puppy, I prayed, "God, would You help this dog be the coolest dog ever, and would You get more glory from him than any other dog ever in history?" I figured it's free to ask God for stuff like that, and it doesn't hurt, so why not? And I think He answered that prayer better than I could have imagined.

Blue ended up knowing more Spanish than most of my friends. Among his favorite words were *vamanos* and *taco*. I'm pretty sure I would have been murdered a couple of times if it wasn't for him. And I would have had to kill a man, too, if it hadn't been for Blue. So, I guess Blue kind of saved that man's life too.

NOT THAT BIG A DEAL

Little did I know that being a youth pastor would be great endurance training for the business I would start later. As a youth pastor, I was constantly criticized and ridiculed for being irresponsible, immature and insensitive. Guilty as charged. I missed a lot of meetings and the kids made messes. Did you know that if you have a race to see which team of 3 teens can chug a 2 liter bottle of soft drink the fastest, they'll all throw up on the carpet? We broke a few windows and pews and doors, but boy did we laugh a lot and have a ton of fun. And lives were forever changed.

That old saying is true, "Where there are no oxen, the stables are clean." I remember early on as the youth pastor, Ronald McDonald pulled me aside, put his hand on my shoulder and said, "You know, Dave, we love you. You're a good man. But we don't want you here, and it'll be better for everyone if you leave." I nodded and thanked him for the kind words and told him I loved him too. Then I smiled and put my hand on his shoulder and said, "You know, Ronald, I believe God called me here, and so I think it's better that I obey Him than you."

That constant criticism and people being mad at me all the time trained me for what was ahead. I don't share all of my opinions publicly in my business, but when I do share one, there's usually someone who acts really upset. One time I shared the Christmas story, out of Luke chapter 2, on our Facebook page, and someone got mad at me for "going religious on us at Christmas." *Ummm* . . .

By February of 1999, I was 27 years old, in debt and burned out. I had no idea what I wanted to do for the rest of my life, and I was tired of being broke and getting chewed out for trying to do the right thing. After 3 years of it, a crack in my armor appeared.

And so, I decided to do what a lot of people do when they don't know what to do next in life. I applied to 4 or 5 graduate schools.

And they all said I couldn't study there.

My backup plan was to return to Multnomah for their Master's program. I figured they'd say yes since they already knew me. I found a youth pastor to move to T or C to take my job, and then prepared to move back to Oregon to start working on my masters in the fall.

Two days before I left, I got a letter from Multnomah also saying that I was not accepted into their graduate program. *What?* They said I didn't have a high enough GPA in my undergrad to be admitted. So, I decided to go to the school in person to explain to them the error in their thinking.

I had only gotten to Albuquerque before my jam packed VW bus was hardly running anymore, which is a common occurrence with those things. Luckily, I found a VW repair shop and walked in with my head hung low. I didn't have a job or much money. This breakdown felt like God was just heaping it on. But I guess that would be like a smoker being mad at God for them getting lung cancer or a parachuter getting mad at God for a broken ankle. I was the one to blame for it. I chose to spend 3 years working at a job that hardly paid anything, and I bought a vehicle that, as part of its charm, is known to break down all the time and I was chock-full of pride.

After a few hours, the owner of the VW shop waved me over and said, "Well, I've got some good news and I've got some bad news for you. The good news is that we'll have you back on the road in a few hours and you should be able to make it to Oregon. The bad news is that it will cost you $850 now and probably $1500 shortly after you get there." It was such a downer.

And that's when the wise shop owner told me something that changed my life forever. He said, "You know, Dave, I bet there are a lot of people out there who would gladly trade your $850 problem for their problem in the snap of a finger. Maybe a mother of 4 little kids who was just diagnosed with terminal cancer, or the family whose home just burned down and almost all of the children got out. Think about it. Relative to what's going on in the world, your $850 problem is not that big a deal."

It took me about 5 seconds to process his words before I raised my chin off my chest, put my shoulders back and handed the man my credit card with a smile. And the card worked too! My problem was a problem, for sure, but in relation to other problems in the world, it was the equivalent of the problem of finding a hair in my food. That little experience shaped who I am today.

When I got to Oregon, I personally went in to ask the fine people on the Multnomah admissions board if they would make an exception and let me in. Right away they said no.

Then I wrote a handwritten letter laying out all the reasons why they should let me in. I explained that college was actually easy for me, that earning a 2.5 GPA in grad school would be no sweat, that I was one of those students who, in my undergrad years, could just go to class and didn't really even need to study and I still got a 2.29 GPA.

No again! Can you believe it?

It turns out the accreditation board required that for an applicant to be accepted, they either had to have an undergraduate GPA of 2.5 or higher or somehow "prove" in the year prior that they could do master's work at that high level.

Looking through the class options, I realized Multnomah offered a one year certificate program that required all the same courses as the first year of the master's program and that program only required a 2.0 GPA to get in. So, I asked the dean of the school, "If I got a 2.5 GPA that year, then could I just continue on to finish up the master's program?" He raised an eyebrow, kind of scratched his head and said, "Interesting. Nobody has ever asked that question. I guess you're in."

FALLING IN LOVE WITH QUALITY

In April of 1999, that recent breakdown in Albuquerque was kind of traumatic for me and caused a life shift. For the first time ever, I had a deep desire for a quality vehicle. Was it too much to ask for a car to be reliable and just work when I needed it to? My dad had bought a 1992 Toyota pickup, brand new off the lot, and that thing just ran and ran and ran without a single problem, and then he sold it with 215,000 miles on it.

I wanted to simplify life by removing the questions, "I wonder when it will break next?" or "How much will it cost this time?" I didn't *just* want something that worked. It had to be well made and reliable. Ideally, I would find something that had a cult following, like my VW Bus had, minus the "charm" of breaking down all the time. This time, my mind was set on trustworthiness, first and foremost. So, I sold the bus and started searching for the perfect vehicle. What reliable and cool looking workhorse could I get with the $3,500 in cash I had in my pocket?

I had wanted an old Toyota Land Cruiser ever since a youth group staff guy, Dave Barnhart, drove me out to go cliff jumping at the Sandy River in his blue FJ40. I knew then and there that one day I would own one. Not only was it a cool rig, but it was designed to never break down. I watched a video of the chief engineer for the Land Cruiser in Japan talking about the company's design philosophy. He explained that they designed and over engineered the Land Cruiser so that if your life ever had to depend on a vehicle, may it depend on a Land Cruiser.

I recently read that on the newer ones, the windshield is 2 millimeters thicker than all other vehicle windshields and the exhaust is double walled with a special stainless steel so nothing will warp if you suddenly go into cold water. The thickness of their camshafts is way over engineered, and the carbon content of their steel is way higher than is necessary. But that's why they say, "You can bend 'em, but you can't break 'em." And I've proven it to be true more than once.

After only a few days, I found the perfect vehicle that checked all the boxes, and some of them twice. It was a 4 door 1971 FJ55 Toyota Land Cruiser and it only cost $1,300. Check, check and CHECK. The Land Cruiser cult affectionately calls it "The Iron Pig." Let me tell you, once you get used to quality, you can never go back. And that's what happened when I bought my first Toyota Land Cruiser.

This was my first step down the road of over engineered quality. Toyota's design philosophy truly influenced my thinking in designing Saddleback Leather goods. One question always on my mind is, "How can I make this design to be the longest lasting, most durable leather piece in the world?" and I think, "If a life needs to depend on a bag one day, may it depend on mine."

Since I still had so much extra money, I started looking around for a roof rack. But not just any roof rack. It had to look just right with the angles and edges of the Land Cruiser, but it had to be sturdy enough for Blue and me to sleep on. I swear I looked everywhere but couldn't find anything like what I was imagining in my head. But I eventually found a man making racks, and so I sketched out the rack I had in my head and he got to work.

And as I walked away from the rackmaker, I remember praying, "God, would You help this rack to be the coolest rack ever?" (It's free to ask, right?) Well, they built it and it came out even better looking than I'd imagined. I even got pulled over a couple of times by strangers asking where they could get one. A few months later, I designed a little ladder to go from the back bumper up to the rack and had a drunk welder build it for me on a trip down in Mexico.

This principle is really important. It's not that *everybody* pulled me over asking where they could get a rack like that, but the 2 guys who did had my exact same taste. If you want to design and sell a product or service, design it for exactly the way you would want it to be *for your own self* and then get it in front of people who have your same tastes. And, of course, if it's going to be for you, you would design it with quality, right? Don't try to go cheap. Successful, recession proof people know that you buy nice or you buy twice, so they're willing to pay a little extra for quality. If you have a choice, and you do, then follow the golden rule of design: *Design unto others as you would have them design unto you.*

Adios America

In Portland, I made a new friend named Jake Miller. We played a lot of ultimate frisbee, and he had an old FJ55 Toyota Land Cruiser too, so we hung out all the time. One night, I went over to his apartment and he was practicing Spanish on the computer. I asked him why, and he told me he'd just signed up to be a volunteer English teacher in Mexico and would be leaving in July.

That sounded so cool. He'd met a man named Brett Hespen who told him they really needed people to help teach English in Southern Mexico for a year, and Jake agreed to go. I said, "Wait! What? Brett's in town? I've got to see him."

Apart from my dad, Brett was my high school youth pastor and happened to be one of the most influential men in my life. To me, he was the absolute coolest guy on the planet. He was fluent in Spanish, played guitar, was a funny and adventurous guy and had six-pack abs. I wanted to be just like him.

When I found him, I gave Brett a big hug and we laughed and got caught up on each other's lives. I told him I knew Jake, and that's when he threw out the invitation to me too. "Hey Dave," he said, "why don't you join us at Centro NOE to teach English for a year? We could really use a guy like you."

Without hesitation, I asked, "When do we leave? Oh wait, I mean, I have to pray about it first, but I think God is going to be cool with it." It was a no brainer, but I always like to check with God first. He likes that, and He's privy to details I'm not always aware of.

I knew this was what I needed to do more than working on my master's. I would become fluent in Spanish, which would open up a lot of doors for ministry later. I would be working with teenagers (always fun), and I would get to eat Mexican food every day. What more did I need to know? The next day I called Brett and committed. The day after that, I waltzed over to Multnomah and thanked them for nothing and told them I didn't want to go out with them anyways.

This was one of the best decisions of my life, even though I lost money that year. Not only was I not making money, but I had to raise $300 a month for living expenses. I'll be forever grateful to our old family friend, Jerry Carver, who chipped in $50 a month, and to the other friends and family members who helped me out too. If someone asks you to support them for something like this, I hope you are fast to help.

GOING DOWN

In July of 1999, Brett, Jake and I took off for Mexico. My folks said they would take care of Blue for the year, and my 16 year old brother swore he would take good care of my Land Cruiser. I dropped Blue and my rig off in New Mexico, packed out an old canvas military duffle bag and my dumpy nylon backpack and we drove on down to Morelia, Michoacan, Mexico. Little did I know that my life was about to get an upgrade.

Living in Morelia was like 7th heaven. I was speaking Spanish, hanging out with teens, surrounded by pretty *señoritas* and eating tacos almost every day. Jake and I found a place selling one peso tacos (about ten cents each at that time) and pigged out. They were mainly tortillas with a little bit of meat, but they sure tasted good with the salsa and cilantro. And did I mention *they only cost one peso?* They were a deal at twice the price, so we ate there all the time.

The director of Centro NOE, Brain Overcast, assessed my Spanish ability and assigned me to teach the 2nd year English students, ages 12 to 17, along with a parents' class in the evenings. That added up to about 25 hours a week. It was my first time formally teaching a class and I really didn't know what I was doing. But just like all of the other newbie teachers who had gone before me, they introduced me to the filing cabinets with all the games and lessons and tests for the daily classes. I also gave guitar lessons and played a lot of basketball with the kids.

On November 1st, against the warnings and pleas of my very churchy host family, I packed my duffle bag with a few things and headed to the "worldly" and "secular" Day of the Dead celebration at the World's center of the festival, just 30 minutes away in Patzcuaro. The graveyards were lit almost to daylight with hundreds of thousands of candles burning on the graves. The relatives of the deceased had decorated the tombs of their loved ones and were waiting for them to come back from the dead, this one night, to partake of their favorite meals and drinks that had been left for them as they made their journey onward. If you've seen the movie *Coco*, you know what I mean. The film's setting was actually inspired by the town I was visiting.

The next day, I saw a tall, smiley white guy about my age crossing the street in front of me. I stood in front of him, stuck my hand out and said, "Hey, I'm Dave. What's your name?"

"Jimmie Jack Drath," he said. He told me he was a seasonal fishing guide from Alaska who was spending the winter in Mexico and was living with a family in Manzanillo, on the coast. After telling him all about how great Morelia was, he went back home, got his stuff and moved there too. And we hung out for the rest of my time in Morelia. You can meet Jimmie, and he'll tell you this same story today, if you happen to go to one of Jimmie Jack's Alaska Fishing Lodges.

WWIJC (WHAT WOULD INDIANA JONES CARRY)?

It was on the Day of the Dead trip when I realized I needed a different bag to travel with. The big green canvas military duffle wasn't cutting it. It was too big, and I had to dig way down in the dark to feel around for whatever I wanted to get out. When I got back to Morelia, I started wandering the markets, looking for just the right bag to travel with, but at the same time, I wanted something I could use to carry my books and the students' papers in too. I wasn't sure what I was looking for, but I just knew I needed something different.

Seeing hundreds of bags I didn't like helped me define more of the look I *did* like. It just so happened Morelia was only a couple of hours away from Leon, in the state of Guanajuato, which was known as the leather capital of North America, and so the markets were filled with leather briefcases and satchels. I knew this bag of mine had to be made of leather. That was a good start.

I must have looked at 300 leather bags over the next couple of weeks, but they all looked like something my dad would carry. No offense, Dad, but I wanted something kind of simple, classic and old fashioned looking, but everything I was finding had a more modern style and had zippers to close them with. Didn't anyone make grandfatherly looking bags with simple buckles anymore? It was a look that, thankfully, was hard to find, and here's why.

When I was in 7th grade, I found Dad's old canvas Chuck Taylor sneakers in his closet, from way back in the day, and thought they were the coolest shoes I had ever seen. The rest of his shoes were regular, uncool leather "dad" shoes like all fathers wore, which were just like the shoes that their fathers and grandfathers had worn before them.

Interestingly, what happened with shoes is the same thing that happened with briefcases. When tennis shoes became popular, it sparked a demand for more casual shoes. As casual shoes became more common, the more people scoffed at anyone wearing shoes like their grandfathers used to wear. So, in the 1960s and '70s, the demand for old fashioned grandfatherly shoes tanked. Sure, people still wore them with suits, but high quality ones for daily wear became hard to find at reasonable prices.

The same thing happened with bags. In the 1960s and '70s, the convenient zipper had become popular and pretty much killed the demand for old fashioned grandfatherly bags with a flap and a buckle. Because zippers could now close a bag, it created a new modern style that intrigued the next couple of generations and drastically lowered the demand for old fashioned bags. And that's why I couldn't find one. I've always kind of been an old soul and was drawn to the classic look of my grandfather's generation, so my search started to feel hopeless.

When I was a kid, my dad used to read me old British novels at night. Since his undergrad was in English Literature, he knew all the good ones. C. S. Lewis' Chronicles of Narnia series and J. R. R. Tolkien's Lord of the Rings trilogy made my imagination run wild. But maybe the most formative books Dad ever read to me were the H. Rider Haggard novels centered around the English adventurer, hunter and explorer Allan Quatermain. He was actually the classic old fashioned character who Indiana Jones was fashioned after.

When Dad took me to see the first Indiana Jones movie, I couldn't believe how cool the guy was, and I wanted to be just like him. In fact, when I was in tenth grade, I went on a mission trip with my youth group to Tijuana, Mexico, and bought a real leather whip at the market, just like the one Indiana Jones carried, and then practiced cracking that whip in the backyard for a solid year. And it didn't stop there. In college, I minored in ancient Greek partly because Indiana Jones was into ancient languages. Isn't it interesting what kind of things shape us?

And then a thought came into my head, and I asked myself, *I wonder what kind of bag Indiana Jones would carry?*

Immediately, I imagined a cool old weathered leather satchel, and the image wouldn't go away. That was it. Indiana Jones was the coolest man ever, and so his bag would have to be too. He was also a university professor, so it needed to have a professional look. But he was also an archeologist, so it needed a flare of ruggedness too. Now I just needed to find someone to make the bag that was floating around in my head.

In El Mercado de Dulces, I found a man named Leonel making leather bags, and asked him in caveman Spanish, "Señor, if me draw bag, you make?"

He smiled and said, "*Sí.*"

So, I drew it out on a piece of paper and then explained it to him. I told him I wanted it to be as basic and as simple as possible, with just a bottom, 4 walls, a flap and a buckle to close it with. And then I wanted a couple of removable belts all the way around the body for just in case situations.

I told him I wanted the bag made with the thickest and strongest leather he could find and lined with a classy suede. And if that weren't enough, I asked him to sew it with the thickest thread his sewing machine could handle. I didn't want any breakable parts either. I told him no zippers, snaps or buttons, because those things eventually break. I was thinking that if the only thing that could break were tough leather and thread, then it should last my whole life.

The daydream I had was this. When I was still warm in the grave, a few of my grandkids would be rummaging through their grandfather's study and would find that bag and start fighting over who got to keep it. The bag had to be unbreakable for that to happen and that dream was where Saddleback Leather's slogan, "They'll Fight Over It When You're Dead," came from.

As I walked away from Leonel's little shop, I asked God, "God, would You make this be the greatest bag to ever exist on Earth, and would You get more glory from this bag than any other leather bag that has ever existed?" Why not ask, right? It doesn't cost anything, and I think God likes to flex when we ask big.

FROM DISAPPOINTMENT TO DELIGHT

In December, we started a long school break. Brett had told us about one of the coolest places in all of Mexico, which was about a 5 hour drive away called Las Grutas de Tolantongo. It's a deep valley in the desert through which flows a warm, baby blue river made up of hot and cold streams with waterfalls oozing out of the caves and pools tucked high up in the valley walls. Since none of us had a car, Jimmie suggested we all wear huge sombreros with colorful *serape* blankets over our shoulders and hitchhike there. He didn't have to suggest it twice.

Leonel was taking forever to build my leather satchel, so I packed up my canvas duffle bag again and we took off. It took us 2 days to get there because one of the families who picked us up insisted we stay the night at their home to celebrate Las Posadas. Las Posadas (The Inns) is a Mexican religious tradition, near Christmas, celebrating the journey of Joseph and Mary looking for an inn to stay in. We walked in a large procession around their neighborhood, knocking on certain doors asking if there was room for us. The people said there was no room in their inn, but they read passages of the Christmas story, sang Christmas songs and gave us refreshments. After a couple of hours and a few houses later, we stopped in one place which was designated as "the stable" and ate the meal. It was a neat experience. Why we don't do stuff like that in our country is a mystery to me.

We stayed the night with them and then hitchhiked on to Las Grutas de Tolantongo the next afternoon. It was shockingly beautiful, way cooler than Brett had told us, but it would have been an even cooler experience if I'd had my new leather bag with me.

On December 28th, 1999, my bag was ready to pick up and I was more than excited. I greeted Leonel in his little leather shop, and he grabbed the bag from underneath his workbench, turned it toward me and smiled. "So, what do you think?"

Right away, I heard in my head the sound of a needle screeching across a record. The bag looked horrible, like something my dad would've carried. Again, no offense, Dad, but it looked like a formal, dark brown monotone and rigid fatherly briefcase. It was not at all the bag I had floating around in my mind.

To say I wasn't very excited about the bag would be like saying I wasn't very excited about getting a tooth pulled. But I widened my eyes and with a fake smile said to the man, *"Es maravilloso! Eres muy talentoso, Leonel. Gracias."* It was the same design and dimensions I gave him and was obviously built like a tank, but it looked as stiff and boring as an old time Baptist preacher.

As I spun it around in my hands, I started to imagine how it could be better, and so asked Leonel if he knew how I could soften the leather up some. He told me to rub lime juice into it and then condition it with a little bit of light oil, like olive or baby oil. On the way home, I picked up those ingredients and some fine sandpaper and got to work.

I started by stomping on it, twisting it and bending it every which way I could. I folded it up and rolled it all over the place until my forearms burned. And it started to soften a little. I then took the sandpaper and began to gently and tastefully remove all of the gloss and some of the paint in places, so it would look naturally weathered. It was starting to get there. I then squeezed and smeared the juice of about a dozen limes all over it and finished it off with some great smelling baby oil and left it to dry. Today, we tell our customers, "Your bag will be the ugliest it will ever be the first day you get it, but put your time in and it'll look better the more you use it."

In the morning, I picked it up, stuffed the colorful little hitchhiking serape blanket in it, set it on the desk and stepped back to look at it. *Bingo!* This was exactly what I'd imagined in my head. Indiana Jones would have been proud, and I couldn't have been prouder. I picked up the satchel, hung it across my chest and started peacocking around the school.

You should have seen my buddy, Jake, when I showed him the bag. His eyes got big, he smiled wide and gave me a high five, but I could tell he was green with envy on the inside. He wanted what I had so bad that he marched right down to the Mercado de Dulces and asked Leonel to make him another one exactly like the one he made for me. Now, I'm not saying that this was the greatest bag to ever exist on Earth. Those would be big words, but it was the greatest bag ever to exist on Earth *for me*.

After using it for a while, I realized it was too simple and needed a few more features, like a pocket for pens and pesos, and so I went back to Leonel and had him put a pocket on the inside. That made it way more useful.

MY BULLFIGHTING CAREER

I loved my new bag and carried it everywhere. I really loved how the thick leather felt. But in February of 2000, I got my first feel of even thicker leather at a Mexican bullfight, and it was still on the bull. Someone invited me to a local university bullfighting fundraiser. It took place in a packed bullring and the energy was intense. Five college students came out riding donkeys and playing polo with brooms and a soccer ball. Everybody laughed and we were all having a good time.

After a bit, the bullring was cleared and the main event was about to begin. Five college students, who were serving as the day's bullfighters, came back into the bullring with their big thick, red capes in hand. Spanish bullfight music started playing and the bull chute opened. Out came running, at full speed, a little Spanish Fighting Bull calf. He seemed angry and clearly intended to take down a matador. Everyone laughed as the bull charged the capes that the students were shaking at him. And every time he charged by, the crowd would yell a hearty *"Olé!"* That baby bull tried his best but tired quickly and was sent back up the chute to fight another day.

The crowd was quiet for a bit, and then a middle school sized bull came rushing out of the chute. The crowd started laughing again, but with their eyebrows raised a little. This bull was definitely bigger and more intense but hadn't grown his horns yet. He, too, charged full speed into the capes and each time the crowd erupted with *"Olé!"* over and over. The young bull also tired out and was ushered back into the chute.

That's when the Spanish guitar and trumpet music started again and softly grew in intensity. It kind of had that *The Good, the Bad and the Ugly* sound. And then, tearing out of the chute charged a fully mature Spanish Fighting Bull, also known as a *Toro Bravo*. A thousand people started oohing and aahing at the trainwreck they saw coming. Things just got real. Right away, the inexperienced and scared to death college students got behind the narrow wooden safety barriers on the edge of the bullring so as to not get ragdolled around the bullring before their time.

These bulls are naturally in a perpetual bad mood and bred specifically for this purpose. To maintain their natural aggressive charm, they're raised on wide open ranches where they rarely, if ever, encounter humans on foot. The best bulls for bullfights are selected based on a combination of aggression, energy, strength and stamina.

This one had all of those characteristics and more. But he had a chip on his shoulder. He had been deemed not good enough to be a *Toro Bravo* because he was "special." You see, he had a perfectly normal curved horn on the left side of his head, but on the right side he had a "lazy" horn. It was straight and kind of sticking out of his head a little at an angle. In the bull world, that lazy horn disqualified him from bullfighting. But even worse, it disqualified him from breeding. And I'm sure it didn't help his self esteem that they always chose someone else instead of him for all the bullring games. It seemed like he knew he was deemed "not good enough" and this was his chance to prove them all wrong.

Right away, one of the students started swinging his hands from side to side and shaking his head, saying something in Spanish over and over again. I wasn't close enough to fully understand what he was saying, but it was something about how he wasn't a man yet but just a little boy and he was scared and he wanted his mommy. Something like that. Anyways, a couple of the other guys tried to talk Chicken Little back into it, but there was no convincing him. He just kept shaking his head as he ran to the exit gate.

On the loudspeaker they announced that they needed a volunteer to take the student's place. I immediately thought to myself, *When will I ever get a chance to fight a bull in a real Mexican bullfight again?* The answer was *never*, and so I stood up and reached my hand to the heavens and started waving it back and forth.

When I looked around, it was quiet and awkward and everyone was just staring at me. Since I was the only one volunteering, they waved me down. I made my way to the wall and jumped down into the bullring. The crowd erupted with cheers and applause. This was going to be so much fun. What could possibly go wrong?

A man handed me the Howard the Coward's abandoned cape and started talking real fast at me. I didn't really understand much of what he was telling me, but from what I gathered, he said to just shake the cape because the bull would go for whatever was shaking.

All 5 of us carefully made our way out from behind the wooden barriers and started shaking our capes and taunting the bull. He looked around at each of us and then, without hesitation, picked me first and charged. The angry bull came barreling toward me, hit the cape and kept on going. All at once, a thousand people cried, *"Olé!"* My adrenaline was flowing like a river. This was my mother's worst nightmare and I'm so glad she wasn't there, but boy was I having a great time.

The second pass was a little different. Actually, it was a lot different. Do you remember the scene when Bugs Bunny fights a bull and the bull stands up, chalks his horns, drops down on all fours, snorts real loud, lowers his head and then kicks some dirt back behind him and charges? Well, this bull didn't stand up or chalk his horns, but he did all the rest without ever losing eye contact with me. And he didn't start running at me slowly either. He charged me from about 30 feet away and reached full intensity in about 1.2 seconds.

Here we go again, I thought. But this time, about ten feet before the bull got to me, he changed his trajectory about ten degrees in the direction of my leg. They said the bull would go after whatever was shaking, and my leg definitely qualified. The bull hit me hard and with all his force. The same people who were crying *"Olé!"* a minute ago were now all gasping as one.

I don't know why I remember that sound so vividly, but it makes me laugh to this day. A thousand people sucking in air, all at the same time, for me. Luckily, the bull hit me square in my abs with the top of his head with his horns on either side. I dropped the cape and, just as he tried to flip me up in the air, I pushed off from his head. I flew a few feet up in the air and landed on my feet off to the side.

But the fun wasn't over yet. The bull whipped right around and was back on me in two seconds flat. I grabbed his horns and pushed off again, and it was right then that the other toreros came rushing in to distract him. It was a good thing too. I didn't want to have to kill him with my bare hands right there in front of everybody. He didn't do anything wrong. He was just being his regular mad self. He was just misunderstood.

Well, that ended my promising bullfight career and it was a good time. All these years later, when I think back about that bullfight, I still pump my fist now and then.

PERFECTING WITH USE

I was using my new bag every day, and that is how I figured out how it could be better. In April of 2000, Jake, Jim and I and a new friend, Ben, had a 2 week break for *Semana Santa* (Holy Week aka Easter), so we decided to take another hitchhiking trip. Before we left, I went back to Leonel to have him put D rings on my bag so I could tie things to it. He put a D ring on each corner of the bottom and a D ring on each corner of the top. This was going to be a epic test for my bag (and me).

We headed east out of Morelia and stuck our thumbs up in the air. It took a little longer this time, because not as many people had room for 4 gringos, but by dinnertime, we'd reached the city of Puebla, which was normally only 7 hours away. Thankfully, the last guy to pick us up was a rich teenager who took us to stay at his family's giant home for the night. His mom and dad weren't very happy with him that he had invited 4 strange men to have dinner and stay the night, but we grew on them and when breakfast was over, we all hugged and they took us to the road that leaves Puebla toward Veracruz.

We started hitchhiking again and it wasn't long before we were at the Gulf of Mexico in Veracruz. Because the air was so thick and sticky, we stayed the night in a hotel and hung out in the city for the day. The new guy, Ben, didn't seem drawn to hitchhiking and decided to turn back after only a few days, but the 3 of us amigos continued on.

Since we didn't have enough money to keep staying in hotels, we caught the overnight bus to Villahermosa, Tabasco, and used the bus as our hotel that night. From there, we continued hitchhiking south to a Mexican state on the Guatemala border called Chiapas. A little after midnight, the driver pulled over in some town called Ocosingo and we jumped out of the back of the pickup and beelined it for a hotel to get showers and some sleep.

That next morning, we 3 clean cut smiley white guys came out of the cheap hotel in search of a cheap meal and everybody was staring at us, but they weren't smiling. At first, we thought we were getting stare points because we were in some random insignificant town where gringos just never visit. But shortly, we learned the real reason.

Only a few years earlier, the oppressed indigenous population of Southern Mexico, led by Subcomandante Marcos, declared war on the Mexican government and they called themselves *Los Zapatistas*. Officially, they were the Zapatista Army of National Liberation (EZLN) and were based out of Chiapas. Ocosingo was the site of a more recent major bloodbath where about 150 Zapatistas and Mexican soldiers were killed in a firefight, some found shot in the back of the head after surrendering. Tensions were still high because it was still unresolved, and the walls of the town were still riddled with bullet holes. One could make the argument for it being the least touristy town on Earth.

Once we realized the significance of where we were, the staring and unfriendliness of the people made sense. The government suspected us of bringing money to or training the rebels, and the rebels thought we were government spies. Why else would any sober gringo, carrying a leather briefcase, visit Ocosingo? So, shortly after our silent and uncomfortable breakfast, we took a taxi to the southern edge of the city and continued hitchhiking.

But Ocosingo wasn't far from where we wanted to be. The massive Mayan ruins of Palenque were breathtaking, and if you looked into the jungle, you could see the majority of the ruins still unexcavated. When we got to the jungle waterfalls of the Cascadas de Agua Azul, we hacked a vine loose from a tree and swung full Tarzan into the river for an hour or two. The place was amazing, and the clear, cold blue river stepped down, creating a series of huge waterfalls.

From there, we hitchhiked our way along the coast of Oaxaca and bought hammocks to sleep between palm trees on the beaches. Hammocks had never been comfortable for me to sleep in because I didn't know how to do it. But in that part of Mexico, pretty much everyone slept in hammocks, and they taught us the trick. You don't sleep right down the middle with your head and feet closest to where it attaches to the trees. You angle your body about 35 degrees off of straight and that lets your body lay flat. I also learned that if you get an extreme sunburn on your back while snorkeling, no angle in a hammock is comfortable for 2 days.

And FYI, that area of the coast of the state of Oaxaca has perhaps the most beautiful beaches in all of Mexico. It's the Cancún of the West Coast but one third the price. From there, we hitchhiked to Acapulco, Ixtapa and Zihuatenejo and then back up to Morelia.

The closer we got to Morelia, the more we longed for our beds back home. The more we rode in the backs of trucks, the more we longed for actual car seats. Nearing the end of the trip, we were standing out by the highway, and I told the guys that I just prayed for God to send us a Mercedes Benz for our next ride. And sure enough, guess what pulled up, a $250,000 Mercedes Benz. But this Mercedes had a crane on the back of it. It was a huge Mercedes Benz work truck, and we had to ride standing up on the flatbed, holding on to the crane for a couple of hours. We got a giant laugh out of that, and I bet God did too. Lesson learned here, it's good to be specific in your prayers.

So how did my bag do? The D rings worked better than planned. By the end of the trip, I had my flippers, mask and snorkel tied to the bottom rings, my serape blanket tied hanging down on one side and my hammock tied to the opposite side. It was my original bag's first big trip, and it easily could have been its last, but we made it through. I loved the D rings and the little pocket for coins. Still, after wear testing it, I learned a few new ways it could get better.

Everybody Wants One

In June of 2000, I had just turned 29 and the school year had just ended, so I headed back up to the US. To say I'd made a pretty good decision to spend my year in Mexico would be an understatement. I left with a lot of new experiences and a better understanding of other cultures and was fluent in Spanish. That year opened doors I never could have imagined, and the education I got in Mexico far outweighed any education I could have gotten at any of the greatest schools of the world. And also, I now owned the leather bag of my dreams.

First things first, I headed back to Mom and Dad's house. I had seen Blue pretty happy before, but never like this. When I called his name, he was a little confused at first, and then he went berserk. And I must say, I was almost in tears. It was such a sweet, sweet reunion. And my little brother had been true to his word and had taken care of my Land Cruiser as if it were his own. Still, it wouldn't start. To this day, he says he can't remember how in the world the starter got so much water in it.

I loved my bag, and it seemed that everybody else did too. I'm not exaggerating when I tell you, back up in Portland, I got at least 3 to 4 compliments or questions about it every single day. Strangers would cross the street or come out of their offices when I walked by their windows. "Excuse me, sir, where did you get that bag?" or "I've been looking for a bag just like that for years! Where do they sell them?" And if they weren't asking about it, they were certainly staring at it.

Even though I got a D minus in accounting, I put two and two together and quickly realized there might be a way to make some money here. If I could just make more bags, then I could sell them and keep working with youth as a volunteer and I wouldn't have to get a real job. This was particularly important to me because I was what I call *psychologically unemployable*. I liked to spell *boss* backwards: double-S-O-B. The only reason I ever wanted a job was for gas so I could go somewhere. At all of my 2 dozen jobs up to that point, I'd always tried to be the best worker they'd ever had, but I was always looking to the horizon wondering where to go next.

By November, while living with Mom and Dad, I had saved up enough money from odd jobs to get back to Mexico. I estimated I had enough money, first for the gas money I would need for the 6,000 mile round trip, and second for getting ten more bags made. So, I quit my job, packed up the old Land Cruiser with a sleeping bag, toolbox, guitar and my dog and started the drive back to Morelia.

As soon as I got there, I negotiated with Leonel to an unbelievably low price to make me ten more bags. He bowed to my skillful bargaining with a smile, and I thought, *Man, I got him so low. How can he do it and still make money?* That was the wrong thinking. And while I was waiting for him to make the bags, I bought $150 of thick black leather to replace the 30 year old vinyl seats in my Land Cruiser and then traded a $149 Craftsman tool set for the upholsterer to do the job. It turned out so cool and was a great deal for both of us.

LESSONS IN THE ART OF NEGOTIATING

Here is how I learned some painful lessons in the art of negotiating, such as: *The goal should not be how low you can get the price.* If it's not a good deal for both of you, then it's not a good deal for anybody.

When I went to pick up the ten bags from Leonel, I couldn't believe my eyes. The leather was orange. Not beige orange, not brown orange, but fairly bright and shiny *orange*. My jaw dropped and my heart sank, and I couldn't believe what he'd done. Leonel had bought a cheaper leather instead of the leather we'd agreed upon for the bags, and I had no choice but to pay the second half of the payment for them and figure out what to do next. And he'd only made 8 of them instead of 10. He'd earned a fair wage, and I walked away with enough gas money to get back to Oregon, and 8 orange bags I had no idea what to do with.

Since I'd negotiated such a low price, I'd forgotten to factor in that people don't work for free. They'll make their money one way or another. In this case, Leonel chose cheaper leather. He wasn't going to make any money at the price I was insisting on, so instead of arguing, he chose a much less expensive leather so he could make money. Actually, the quality of the leather was not lower, it was just ugly. It was probably a leather the vendor was overjoyed to finally sell.

In the manufacturing world, we say, "You can choose 2 of these 3 things: low price, on time delivery or high quality, but you can't have all 3." If you choose low price and high quality, they'll work on it when they have extra time between projects. If you choose low price and on time delivery, the quality won't be there. If you choose high quality and on time delivery, the price won't be low.

It was time to solve the ugly leather problem. Nobody was going to want orange bags. While I was still in Morelia, I used Brett Hespen's belt sander and got most of the orange off. Then I took some fine grit sandpaper and hand sanded around the stitching, in an uneven kind of way. All of this took forever, but I was making progress.

After a month in Mexico, I headed up to my sister Jeanne's house in Texas and camped out on her couch for a few days while I figured out what to do with the 8 bags. They had the right shape but looked pretty rough with the pale whitish orangish leather. And that's when it struck me. Of course! Shoe polish. It's made for leather and they have all kinds of colors. I used to polish my dad's boots when I was a kid, and I always used the color of polish that matched the color of boot leather. So, I went to the store, bought dark brown shoe polish and started artfully staining the bags. It took a lot of time but was strangely satisfying. It was as if I were creating 8 beautiful works of art. They actually turned out nicer looking than I had hoped.

So this guy named Tim, who got my sister pregnant 4 *times*, felt sorry for me and bought one of the bags, then quietly tucked it away into the top of the hall closet and left it there. Kind of like keeping a beautiful racehorse in a garage or an eagle in a cage. But I didn't know he did that until later, but I sure was grateful. What a great brother-in-law! Now I had $250 in my pocket.

MY THIRD GRADE MARKETING EFFORT

It was December 15th, and people were in buying mode for Christmas, so I knew I had to get up to Portland before I missed the rush. But I had a thought: *Why not take advantage of the whole trip back to Portland as a chance to sell these bags? I'm guaranteed to not sell a single one if I don't try, so why not try?*

I printed out two 8.5" x 11" sheets of paper with the big words "Real Cool Leather Bags For Sale." I taped one of the signs on the left rear side window and one on the back. The reason I put it on the left side is because, though that Land Cruiser could pull the state of Texas behind it, its comfortable max speed was 55 mph and therefore all vehicles would be passing me on the left. Sometimes, it's those little details that make all the difference.

So Blue and I jumped into my old faithful Land Cruiser with 7 leather bags left and slowly headed northwest to Portland, Oregon. It was late by the time we rolled into the Walmart parking lot in Amarillo, and I needed some sunflower seeds and caffeine to keep me awake. I went in, and to my surprise, when I came out, there was a big dually pickup truck parked behind the Land Cruiser and Blue was barking his head off through the window.

I got up to the truck and a friendly couple stepped out to talk. The lady said, "We were driving by and that sign in the back window caught our attention. We tried to look in, but your dog was barking so much we couldn't see anything. Do you mind if we take a look at your 'real cool leather bags'?"

After holding and feeling it and hearing the story, they said they just had to have it. They asked how much and I told them $250. They asked if I would take a check and I told them it would have to be cash. They said they had to go to an ATM for the money, but I wondered if they would come back. Was my price too high? But they came back and gave me the money. I thanked them and then, with my chin high and chest out, confidently marched right back into Walmart to buy some beef jerky and other celebratory foods. That was huge confirmation to me that I was onto something special with these bags, and I was riding high.

I love exploring and seeing new places and since I had so much money now, I figured I would spend a little extra on gas and drive a new route up through Colorado and then west through Wyoming in the middle of December with a broken heater. What could possibly go wrong?

At about 2 a.m. in Wyoming, they closed the highway behind me because of the ice storm. It was 8°F and the roads were icy, but since I was driving an invincible 4 wheel drive Toyota Land Cruiser equipped with none other than BF Goodrich All Terrain tires, what did I have to worry about? They were the best tires money could buy for my Land Cruiser, and I thought I was unstoppable, until I wasn't.

I knew not to slam on the brakes when your car starts sliding on ice. In fact, each year when it first snowed, I would practice stopping to get used to it. Still, when the Land Cruiser started sliding to the side, instinct took over and I slammed on the brakes and started spinning even more.

We hit the median at about 50 mph, going perfectly sideways, slid for a bit through the snow and then *slammed* over onto the driver's side. We would have rolled all the way over and scratched the roof, but I had that heavy duty rack mounted to the top and that dropped us back down onto the driver's side.

The 1971 Land Cruiser didn't have seatbelts, so it hurt pretty good. After we came to rest, I called for Blue, but everything was silent. When I picked him up in my arms, his body was limp, his head hung straight down and his tongue was hanging down out of his mouth. I think my big metal toolbox had hit him.

I started screaming to God: *"No, God! Please, God, help! Don't let him be dead. Bring him back, God! Please! Help!"* I prayed like my life depended on it. Right away, Blue's eyes opened. His head raised, he pulled his tongue in and started wagging his tail.

After the tow truck driver pulled us back onto all fours, Old Faithful started right up and we drove on slowly to Rock Springs to get a warm bath and some good sleep. In the morning, I surveyed the damage. The side view mirror had broken off and the rack was a little bent, but that was about it. The worst thing about it all was that Blue's whole bag of dog food had spilled out and it took forever to clean up.

On December 19th, we finally rolled into Portland, but I had no idea how I was going to sell the remaining 6 bags. I carried a couple of the bags around the crowded Clackamas Town Center mall, hoping someone would stop me to ask about them, but nope, nothing. Mom, Dad and my little brother, Jonathan, had moved back to Portland too, so Jonathan and I went to Washington Square mall to do the same thing.

Sure enough, a guy selling novelty art kits in a kiosk said, "Hey, those are really cool bags. Would you be up for trading one for some of these art kits I'm selling?"

Bingo. Christmas shopping for my nieces and nephews was done and I started feeling a little more encouraged. Selling leather bags wasn't as easy as I'd imagined it would be, but I was hopeful.

The next day, I parked up on NW 23rd, also known as Trendy Third, to sell the remaining 5 bags. It was in the artsy fartsy part of town, filled with rich people stores, doggie spas and quaint little cafes. And it was packed with last minute Christmas shoppers too. As per usual, I let down the tailgate, spread out the Mexican blanket for Blue to lay on and hung the bags off the side of the rack. I then moved the "Real Cool Leather Bags For Sale" sign to the sidewalk side of the Land Cruiser and just stood there.

Five minutes hadn't even gone by before a man stopped to ask me how much the bags were. He went straight away to an ATM for his $250 cash and walked away with a new bag. After about an hour and a half, I had sold all 5 bags. I had $1,250 cash in my pocket, a grin on my face and a tank full of steam.

To Murder My Assassin

In January of 2001, I knew I needed to get back to Mexico to get more bags, but I also knew I didn't have enough money to get more than just a few. Should I stay in cold and rainy Portland, get a job, save enough money to go to Mexico to buy more bags, or should I move to warm and sunny Mexico, get a job, eat tacos every day and have a local leather craftsman make some bags while I worked? Well, that was an easy decision.

And then I thought, *If I'm going to live in Mexico, why not live where people go on vacation?* Surely there were leather craftsmen in those places too. I had driven to Mazatlan and Puerto Vallarta before and also hitchhiked through Acapulco, so the decision was between one of those towns. I booted up Dad's computer with dial up internet and started looking for a job in Mexico.

It wasn't long before I found a hotel in Acapulco that needed someone just like me. They said they would pay me to wander around Acapulco, strike up conversations with complete strangers and give them free dinners and tours if they would visit the Mayan Palace to hear a 60 minute presentation about their timeshares.

My mom said it sounded too good to be true, but I still hadn't learned the "then it's probably not" part of that lesson yet. I packed a suitcase full of clothes, swim trunks, the toolbox, sleeping bag, duct tape, Leatherman tool, fishing pole, my guitar and my original leather bag, and Mom and Dad hugged my neck and scratched Blue goodbye.

WORKING IN MEXICO

We finally got to Acapulco, and the Mayan Palace guys couldn't believe I'd actually shown up. They set me up with a free apartment with a beautiful view of the city. The reason it had such a view was because it was on the fifth floor of a building with only stairs. Even Blue didn't like it. My next-door neighbor, Steve, was a really nice alcoholic. He was a pit boss from Las Vegas who was having someone illegally collect and deposit his unemployment checks for him so he could live the life on the beach. He was a walking chimney who always had a cigarette in his mouth, and I mean *always*.

The job was cool at first and I got quite a few people to go to the timeshare presentation, but it only took about a week for me to start hating it. When I would approach people, some would roll their eyes and tell me that I was bothering them on their vacation. That, combined with the fact that I couldn't find a leather craftsman in all of Acapulco, was all I needed to know to get out of there as soon as I found something else.

After about 5 sweaty weeks working for the Mayan Palace, I asked my new friend, Pepe Catalan, if he knew of any other job I could do because I absolutely hated this one. He said he was recently invited to teach golf to tourists at a new golf resort a few hours north of Acapulco and said I could go with him to see if there was something they might hire me for too. So, I asked my Vegas pit boss neighbor to watch Blue, and Pepe and I took the early bus to a town up in the mountains called Real de Trece.

There I am sitting in front of the real estate sales manager, Rolando Mota, and he asks me, "So, do you know how to sell real estate?" With a slightly insulted look on my face, I rolled my eyes and laughed and said, "Is the Pope Catholic? Of course I do!" And that was the start of me learning how to sell real estate. The next day, I quit my job, packed up our stuff, and Pepe, Blue and I drove to Real de Trece.

Real de Trece was an unusually comfortable place to live. The combination of 6,500 feet in elevation and 20 degrees North latitude made it a very constant 68 to 75°F all year round. It was lush and mountainous and known as Mexico's primary flower growing region.

Add to the perfect weather the huge amusement park, spa and really nice new golf course, makes Real a big tourist destination for people from Mexico City. The only Americans I knew within 45 miles were a missionary family in town, a 75 year old lady from New York and an old man with dementia selling wine. I felt bad for him, but my pride kept me thinking more about my own self than about the self of others, so I didn't bother to help him. I have messed up plenty, but this is one of the big regrets I have in life. I'm sure his family always wondered where he'd wandered off to and where he was laid to rest. Maybe they'll read this book and finally be at peace.

I'm not going to name the family I worked for, but the 2 dons of the family owned the town. Not Don, as in short for Donald, but rather "don" as in the patriarch or the oldest generation of males in a family. My brother and I won't become dons until Dad dies. Right now, Dad would be "Don Herberto" in a Spanish speaking country. I'm still just "Señor Dave."

All that happened, or didn't happen, in that town was determined by the family. Just before I arrived, they said someone had tried to open up a drug rehab facility in the town, against the will of the family, so they sent one of their bulldozers in at night and leveled the building.

The two brothers couldn't have been more different. One owned the amusement park and was kind and caring and married to one of the most delightful and classy women in the state. And their kids were carbon copies of them, friendly and likable too.

But I worked for the other brother. He was as friendly as a seasick crocodile, and in my whole 2 years there, I never once saw him smile. I probably wouldn't have smiled either if I had a wife like his. She always had an angry look on her face and was mean to everyone. There was an elevator in the hotel and when the door opened for her, if there was someone in it, she made them get off so she wouldn't have to ride with someone lesser than herself.

The don I worked for was connected to everyone who was anyone powerful in Mexico. Daily, we saw lots of bodyguards, automatic weapons and super corrupt looking politicians coming through. And they all had bulletproof vehicles. Near the end of my time there, the police chief of Mexico City became their head of security. We all had questions about things going on but realized it was best just to not ask them.

I found a little $65 a month apartment to rent in an old walled hacienda along the main street. It was charming, in a Clint Eastwood Spaghetti Western sort of way. Imagine the final gunfight in an old Mexican town, and when the smoke and dust clear, there are dead bodies hanging out of broken windows and the walls are riddled with bullet holes. Well, minus the dead bodies, my apartment looked like that. They must have dragged the dead bodies away just before I got there.

My apartment was a big, bare room with maybe half of the windows broken out. There was a bare and empty 7' x 12' room off the side for a kitchen, and a bathroom with a functioning electrical outlet about 2 feet directly below the showerhead (I'm not kidding). There was a sink half hanging off the wall and there was a toilet, but sadly, there wasn't a toilet seat. But you get used to that. I bought an old mattress and laid it on the floor, and I sunk a bunch of nails into the walls to hang my clothes. But the door locked, and Blue had room to roam around the walled hacienda.

By April, everyone in town knew Blue. As we'd drive down the main street, he would usually hang his head out the window and bark and bark to announce our coming. Everybody would smile and wave and shout, "*Hola*, Blue! *Hola*, Blue!"

And just about every night, Blue and I could be found at our favorite fine dining establishment. I'd park the Land Cruiser right in front so Blue could lie on the Mexican blanket on the tailgate and stare at them cooking and cutting the al pastor meat off the spire out front. The 2 brothers had the best tacos al pastor in town, and almost every night I would order 6 of them with one tortilla and a slice of pineapple and then put on cilantro, lime, salt and their amazing red salsa made with Chile Serrano. And I always told them, *"Sin cebolla, por favor."* (That means "No onion, please.") I hate onions so much that I wish all of them would burn in Hell forever. I think they're the dumbest looking vegetable there is, and the sound of the word hurts my ears. Did you know that at least 10 percent of people are like me and hate onions? I've taken polls at taco stands and in restaurants. It's the truth.

One night, one of the taquero brothers told me that his wife and kids, who also worked at the taco restaurant, were talking about how one day they wanted to have a dog just like Blue. Well, I had an idea. I had just studded Blue out to someone whose bitch was in heat. And in Mexico, the stud fee is this: If there are 5 or fewer puppies, then they choose one to give me. If there are 6 or more, then they give me one and I choose one. Well, Frida was pregnant and I was going to get a puppy pretty soon. So, I proposed to Luis: to trade a puppy for tacos. The agreement we came to was he would give me 100 tacos and I would give him one Labrador puppy. It was a win win win deal for Luis, me and Blue.

And luckily for Blue, the word had gotten around among all of the female Labrador owners that there was a new stud in town. If there's inbreeding, then Labs get bad hips and short legs. So Blue was popular because he was injecting new DNA into the Labrador breed of Mexico. And Blue didn't mind. It was his pleasure to serve.

THE EXPERT UPGRADE

By August, I had saved up enough money to get some more bags made, but there wasn't a soul in the Real area who knew anything about leather. As I was asking around, everyone told me of Leon, a town 8 hours away where there was a tannery on every corner and leather workers flowed like beer. Arriving in Leon, I started asking strangers, "Excuse me, do you know where I could find a good leather worker?" and everyone pointed me in the direction of an old man named Don David.

Don David had a big, wide smile and gentle sparkling eyes that put me at ease right away. I handed him my bag and asked if he could make one like it. That was a dumb question. He could have made a leather spaceship if I would have asked him. His father's father was a leather craftsman in that same workshop back in the late 1800s. And so, his grandfather trained his father who in turn trained him. Don David had started as his father's full time apprentice in 1948 at the ripe old age of 10 and was now training his son, Mauricio, to one day take his place too.

So I gave Don David a deposit to make 5 bags, sat on an overturned 5 gallon bucket and we completely redesigned the bag. I'd walked with the original for almost 2 years and knew exactly what it was missing and what needed to change. And Don David had repaired so many leather bags through the decades, he knew exactly what would eventually tear and wear out, and how to construct and reinforce it so it wouldn't.

I added a divider so we had a front and rear section. He said we would need to reinforce the bottom of the bag with an extra piece of leather, so I asked him to only sew it on 1 side instead of all 4. *Voilà*, a false bottom to hide things under. He also surprised me with a super comfortable handle that had hidden reinforcing polyester straps so the leather wouldn't stretch and eventually tear. We added two outer side pockets and two on the inside and then two flat interior side pockets for pens. I wanted to be able to convert it into a backpack, so I designed it with a detachable strap to pass through a center O ring right behind the handle, and he reinforced the D rings on the bottom rear of the bag to attach it to. I didn't know how to design a comfortable yet functional shoulder pad, but Don David did and made it without me even asking.

I drove back to Real de Trece after a week in Leon, with the bags being made and filled with energy and excitement. It was finally happening, and I could get more bags made so I could get back to working with youth. The trip was above and beyond what I'd ever asked God for or even dreamed of, but little did I know what was about to happen and how it would put things on hold.

Early on the morning of September 11th, 2001, everything came screeching to a halt. I came into the clubhouse at the golf course and watched on TV the smoking Twin Towers in New York City and what followed. By the end of the week, the country club was a ghost town. Nobody was traveling, and certainly nobody was looking for a nice lot to invest in on a golf course.

As fate would have it, my taquero friend claimed his new puppy was stolen. At the same time, I was getting another stud fee puppy from a different Lab, also named Frida. In his time in Mexico, Blue had 3 "special friends" named Frida, and for years, he wagged his tail hard every time I would say the name "Frida." We agreed on the same deal as before, one puppy for 100 tacos. It worked out well because money was starting to get tight, and I needed to eat.

In March of 2002, my sister Jeanne was really into eBay and was selling everything in her house that wasn't nailed or screwed down. And one of those things was that original leather bag they so kindly bought from me and tucked away. So, Jeanne asked if it would bother me if she sold that leather bag on eBay because "it just doesn't work for Tim." I told her it was fine and it didn't bother me a bit. I even volunteered to visit and write a little story about how the bag came into being, that may help her get a little more money for it.

So I wrote the eBay description, in basically one big, long paragraph, telling a few fun stories and explaining what Don David taught me about quality construction and materials. She posted the bag for a 7 day auction, and we couldn't believe what happened. The encouraging messages and comments came flooding in about the bag. When it sold for $335, we all laughed and high fived and hugged. And then it got quiet and we looked around at each other. What just happened? We stood there stunned. I will never forget that wonderful feeling. Getting more bags was all I could think about for the next few months. Every day, all day long.

MEETING MY ASSASSIN

When I got back to Mexico at the end of March, I was thinking more seriously about how I was going to survive. I had 5 bags in Leon that were half paid for, but nobody was buying land at the country club. But there was another deal I was a part of. A couple of businessmen from Mexico City were looking for a large piece of land to build a Jewish kosher resort on. They had looked at the land inside of the country club walls, but it was way too expensive.

A year or so earlier, a man named Juan Diablo approached me and offered a 10 percent commission if I could sell any of his land. When he was working in government, he said he and others would leave the office every day with at least $1,000 USD cash in their pockets. So as not to look suspicious by depositing it in the bank, he bought land instead. He owned 1000s of acres and now wanted to turn some of that land back into cash.

I was living in a small home in a quaint little 300 person town called Titomatepec, where Juan lived, about 3 miles outside of Real de Trece. So, I had spent quite a bit of time with him and trusted him about as far as I could throw him. People talked about all the suspicious activities going on under the blue tarps at his house, and I caught him lying all the time. He had a bad temper and would stiffen up like Yosemite Sam and get really intense and talk through clenched teeth when he was mad. Then he would start to shake. It was pretty funny to see.

Juan told me he was so afraid of getting caught for stealing all of that money that he lived like a poor man so nobody would ever suspect him of corruption and investigate. I pulled up the dirt road to his house outside of town one time and he was out in the dirt standing in his boxers in a big washtub, and his wife was sponge bathing him. His home had concrete floors with crumbling walls and chickens everywhere. It's just like that with so many of our politicians who steal so much money today. They have it but can never use much of it or let anybody know they have it. I think it's funny.

Well, the businessmen were looking for about 40 acres and Juan had the perfect land right on the edge of town. A week later, they came to see it and said it was just right, and the price of $10,000 per acre in such a tourist destination was incredible.

I went back and forth to their offices in Mexico City to work out the details of the deal and was close to finalizing the sale. I was sure not to mention anything to Rolando, my boss at the country club, because I knew he would try to worm his way into the deal somehow or even try to take it over. But with all my trips to Mexico City, he started suspecting a sale was going down behind his back.

I eventually told him about it, and he said, "Of course, when they buy, I'll get a commission too, right?" When I mentioned to Juan that Rolando wanted a commission, he smiled and slid two fingers across his throat and said, "Don't worry about Rolando. I'll just have him killed." It looked like the only cut from the deal Rolando would get would be the one across his jugular. So, I casually said to Juan, "That's interesting. How does that happen?" Juan went on to explain that he knows some *federales* (members of the federal police force) who will pour alcohol all over Rolando and throw him in front of a semi-truck on the highway in the middle of the night so it will look like he'd stumbled out onto the highway, drunk.

"So," I calmly asked, "how much does something like that cost?"

"Usually about 3,000 American dollars," he said.

The word *usually* really bothered me. So, that's when I did the math and started thinking about my own neck as well as Rolando's. Let's see, I was about to be owed a $40,000 commission by a guy who hires hitmen for $3,000 so he doesn't have to pay commissions. Hmm...

And that's when I got the bright idea of getting Juan to sign a contract. I wrote into it that he owed me 10 percent of any sale of any land between the Jewish group and him. It also said that if I were not around or alive to collect it, then any family member or any of the dozen friends listed on the contract could come and collect it on my behalf.

I went early the next Friday to ask him to sign the contract, and with a sad and disappointed look he said, "What? You mean you don't trust me? I thought we were friends." He tried the "My word is my bond" line and more. Then suddenly he told me he had to leave because he'd just realized he was late for something. *Are you kidding me?* Being late had never bothered him before. He was late for everything. But I would have to catch up with him later to get his signature.

The next evening, there was a big wedding celebration going on down the street from my home, so I pulled the Land Cruiser up to the edge of the party and stepped out to celebrate with them.

At about midnight, I looked over my shoulder only to see one of Juan's teenage sons about 50 feet away, pointing me out with his finger to a gorilla shaped man next to him. I smiled and waved at them. The boy took off and the man marched straight over to me. I had never seen his face before, but I promise you now, I'll never forget it. He was about 5' 10" and weighed a solid 220 pounds.

He tapped me on the shoulder and immediately introduced himself as Jacobo. He put a six-pack of cheap Mexican beer on the tailgate of my Land Cruiser and offered me one. I accepted. Right away, he told me he was a *federale* and all about how he'd been in the Mexican special forces and how he had been shot many times. He had pictures and everything. He even lifted his shirt up and showed me bullet hole scars in his ribs and shoulder, front and back.

About 20 minutes into our conversation, he signaled with his hand for me to wait, then pulled out a small baggie of cocaine, dipped his coke nail in and snorted it up. And then he resumed our conversation as if nothing had just happened. Then he offered me another warm beer. I said, "*Gracias*, but no. I'm about to head back to hit the sack, and a second beer this late would give me heartburn and keep me awake."

He kind of squinted his eyes and through clenched teeth said, "Do you want me to kill you right now? Take a beer!" I can't remember the brand, but I don't know if I've ever had a better tasting warm beer in my life.

In our conversation, without me saying a word, he casually brought up the expiration date of my Mexican work visa. No one knew that but me. And then he mentioned, by name, some of my friends in a town 45 minutes away. And that's when I started praying.

Then he asked how well I knew Juan and asked if he would be good to pay him if he did something for him. I rolled my eyes, shook my head and laughed. "Juan Diablo? That guy owes everybody money. He's a big talker, but you can't trust him. Sure, he's land rich, but cash poor. The only money he gets is from cockfighting." I mean, I threw out everything I could.

About then, he looked up at the safari rack on my Land Cruiser and asked, "This rig looks like it belongs in Africa. Have you ever been there?" I told him no, but that I really wanted to go one day. He went on to tell me that he also really wanted to go but didn't have anyone to go with. He'd tried posting in forums for someone to go with, but hadn't had any luck. That's when I said, "No way! That's crazy, I've been wanting to go to Africa for years too, but didn't have anyone to go with either. What are the chances of that? Why don't we go together?" He looked at me and smiled. It was at that point I knew we were becoming amigos.

And right then is when the "Blue effect" kicked in. Blue had been resting in the front seat but hopped into the back where we were, almost on cue, and laid down on the tailgate. Jacobo looked at him, then looked at me and then paused to think. "Is your dog's name Blue?"

"Yes," I responded.

He smiled and said, "Then you know my sister, Lupita?"

"Of course I know Lupita," I responded as I nodded my head, smiling, trying to think of who Lupita could be.

"My sister told me a few weeks ago that while she was in Real de Trece, she met a gringo who she really liked, and he had the most handsome and well trained black Lab she had ever seen." And that's when the lightbulb went off in my head and I remembered who Lupita was.

Blue and I had been at the main square a few weeks back, eating an ice cream cone, when 3 young *señoritas* came up to Blue and started gushing over him. They were doing a weeklong college internship at the resort I was working at, and so we started talking. One of them just wanted to hang out with Blue. As I asked about her family, she told me she had a seriously messed up brother named Jacobo who was on the federal police force. She told me how tough and miserable his life was and that he had a horrible drug addiction. She said he had even tried to commit suicide several times. Oh, that sister.

I told Jacobo, "You know, I was meaning to call Lupita, because it's not every day you meet such a woman as her. Who knows, we could even be brothers-in-law one day." And we toasted our cheap warm beers. *"Salud!"*

By about 2:30 a.m. the party was winding down and the crowd had thinned out, and that's when I fake yawned real big, stretched my arms up to the heavens and said, "Well, it's pretty much time for me to go. I've got a long day tomorrow, with church and all, so I've got to get going. You take care, my friend, and let's keep in touch so we can plan that trip to Africa. *Buenas noches*, brother-in-law."

He looked back at me with a serious look on his face and said, "No, I need you to take me to where I'll be sleeping in Real tonight. Let's go."

I thought for a second and said, "How about we get you a taxi?"

He looked me in the eyes and slowly said a second time, "Do you want me to kill you right now?"

I guess nobody told him that threatening to murder someone you just met is not a good way to establish a lasting friendship.

PLANNING HIS MURDER

I told him it was no problem for me to take him into town since there weren't any taxis around at this late hour, but I just needed a few minutes to clear some space for him to sit in the front seat. I really just needed time to set up his murder.

I didn't really want to kill Jacobo, but I didn't have a choice. It was either him or me. This was my plan. Since the Land Cruiser had a big bumper that stuck out about a foot and there were no seatbelts, I was going to crash it into a tree at about 15 mph along the dark highway heading back to Real. I would brace for the planned impact but he wouldn't. Then, I would grab the hatchet that I'd just secured in place by my side, run around to his side of the car and hatchet him in the head as hard as I could, over and over again, until he was dead.

I always kept that hatchet sharp, just in case. As John Wooden, the all time winningest coach of NCAA basketball would say, "When opportunity presents itself, it's too late to prepare." I never thought it would be for such a grisly deed as this, but it was ready to go.

Then a simpler plan struck me. If my Toyota wouldn't start, then I couldn't drive him and then he would just have to leave. Quickly, I reached under the dashboard and pulled out as many fuses as I could, as fast as I could. As he opened the door, I slipped the 7 or 8 fuses into my shirt pocket and turned the key. And, as all Toyotas do, she started right up. *Seriously?* I'd pulled out every fuse *except* the ones that kept the car running. My dash lights didn't work, the dome light didn't come on when he opened the door and I'm sure I'd pulled the windshield wiper fuse too. I couldn't believe it.

Before we headed back to Real, he said he wanted to stop by Juan's place for a few minutes. I suggested he get one of Juan's boys to take him to town, but he ignored me. He was inside Juan's home for about 15 minutes, and I used that time to pray more and also to think through the murder plan better.

Okay, so I kill him. Then what? He's a *federale*. At that time, when a police officer was killed in Mexico, it started a major manhunt, sometimes on a national level. All police stood behind the death of any law enforcement officer, local or federal, and they stopped at nothing to avenge their death. My friend told me in Morelia, someone killed a cop and the whole police force cornered the killer in a canyon outside of town. When they found the body, it had more than 200 bullet holes in it.

Well, I didn't want 200 bullet holes in me, so I had to figure out how to give myself some time to leave Mexico casually without becoming a suspect. If they ever found his body, they would know it was me because I was the last one to be seen with him and I wouldn't be safe, not even in the States. I had to bury the body in a remote place. But then what about when they did find him? They would check his dental records. Umm . . . I'm not going to share the next steps I had planned.

It was 3 a.m. when we started down that dark and empty highway. Jacobo then declares that he was hungry and that we were going to get some tacos before I dropped him off, so I decided not to crash just yet. In Mexico, it's not hard to find taco stands on weekends open that late. We went in and Jacobo told me to drink another beer. Again, when I told him that I had already had too much because I was driving, he leaned across the table and quietly told me those same words again, through clenched teeth: "Do you want me to kill you right now?"

For tacos to be my last meal would have been very appropriate. It's what I would choose over a filet mignon or fancy salmon dish any day. As we sat there, at either his or my last supper, I started to probe into his pains based on what his sister, Lupita, had told me. Jacobo told me about his hurts and sorrows and even teared up a few times. I felt really bad for him, because his heart was hurting so badly, and he didn't know what to do to make it feel better, but I did.

We finished the meal and I told him I didn't have any money and that he had to pay. So he paid and we hopped back into the Land Cruiser to take him to where he was going to sleep. He directed me randomly down one street and then up another and then suddenly told me to stop. He got out at some obviously random casa, walked up to the dark front door and then after 10 seconds came back and said, "No one was there. I'm sleeping at your house."

I told him I didn't have room and the owners asked me not to have guests. He told me he knew I had 2 beds and demanded I take him back to Titomatepec. This was going to be interesting.

SAVING MY ASSASSIN

As soon as we parked, he got out, snorted some more cocaine next to the house and then we went inside. After talking for a time, he sat down on one of the single beds and I sat facing him on the parallel bed 2 feet away. And that's when I asked him, "Jacobo, are you looking for peace in your life?"

"*Sí!*" he said, as he was nodding his head firmly with tears in his eyes.

"Are you looking for joy in your life?"

"*Sí!*"

"Are you looking for love and to be loved?"

"*Sí! Sí!*"

"Jacobo, you can look your whole life and find some of that here and there in temporary things and people and situations, but they fade. You can have all those things right now through a personal relationship with God. And you can only get to God through Jesus. He loves you and is pursuing you and deeply desires a close friendship with you. And as soon as you start that relationship, then all the bad things you've ever done will all be permanently erased from your record. Forgiven once and for all. And even the bad things you'll do in the future will be forgiven at that moment too."

He had a desperate look in his eyes and asked, "What do I have to do to get that?"

"It's simple," I said. "All God wants is that we believe Him. He said that Jesus died on the cross to pay for our sins so we wouldn't have to pay for them. Then, He was buried and He was raised alive after 3 days. And He did all of that because He loved us so much and wanted us to be in Heaven with Him forever. He wants us to believe deep down in our hearts that whatever He says is true. He wants us to trust Him. To put our faith in Him. It's that simple."

When I die and I'm standing in front of God and if He were to say to me, "Hey, Dave! Great to see you. But tell me why I should let you pass through these pearly gates into Heaven." I would tell Him,

"Well, You told me that Jesus died on the cross to pay for all of my sins, and then He was buried and then on the third day He was raised from the dead. I believed You with all my heart. I was counting on that being true. That's all I've got."

As soon as we believe that, and are counting on it, then we are called "believers" and we become a child of God and start that personal relationship with Him, and all of the bad things we've ever done are completely and permanently wiped off our record. As I was sharing the good message with him, aka the gospel of Jesus, it was obvious the cocaine was making him fidgety and distracted. He was looking left and right and then back at me, and it was hard to keep his attention.

So I stopped and said, "Hey, Jacobo, will you read through this little booklet with me called the Four Spiritual Laws (but in Spanish)? I'll read the regular print and you read the bold print, okay?"

He nodded and we started reading out loud together.

I basically said, "God has a plan for us: a life together with Him forever. But we have a problem, and it's called *sin* and it separates us from God."

Jacobo looked up at me and nodded his head firmly on that part. I explained to him, "There is a big sin canyon between us and God, and we try to get to God by being good enough or by going to church or by tithing or a number of things. But it's impossible for us to get to God on our own, because our sin separates us from Him. The Bible says that everyone has sinned and so we all fall short of getting to God."

He was right there with me and nodded his head with a desperate look in his eyes.

So I continued, "But God has a solution to our sin problem. The Bible says that God sent Jesus to die on the cross to pay the debt for our sins so that we wouldn't have to die spiritually to pay for it. Jesus made a bridge across that canyon. Jesus said, 'I am the way, the truth and the life. No one comes to the Father except through Me.'"

Jacobo nodded again.

Then I told him, "It's called grace. Grace is a free gift that we don't earn or deserve. The payment for our sin is something we didn't deserve or earn either. It's just a free gift. And He's sticking it out in front of us to take. But we need to accept that gift. We need to receive it."

So he says to me, "That's what I want. What do I have to do to accept the gift so my sins will be paid for?"

"Just believe in Jesus," I told him. "That's all God wants. God said that His son paid for all of our sins so we wouldn't have to pay for them. He just wants us to trust Him that it's true. He wants us to believe Him with our whole heart. To put our faith in Him. To know that whatever He says is true."

I wasn't sure if it was the cocaine distracting Jacobo or if it's just that he didn't really get it, so I gave him some examples, but it was obvious he was not fully getting it until I did.

So I said, "A long time ago, there was a man named Abraham. He was 75 years old, and he and his wife still didn't have any kids. But God told him, 'Abraham, look up at the stars in the heavens. You're going to have more descendants than all the stars that you can count here.' I imagine maybe Abraham pumped his fist and said, 'Yes! I'm finally going to have some kids! Right on!' And the Bible said, 'And Abraham believed God and it was put on his account as righteous' (or 'right before God')."

Then I asked him, "Do you know the story about *Noe y la Arca*?" He nodded, but I didn't think he really knew it very well. So, I told him that story too.

"God came to Noah and said, 'There's going to be something called rain, and then a thing called a flood, so you'll need to build what's called a boat.' I'm sure Noah didn't understand, but he trusted that what God said was true. The Bible says that because of Noah's faith, because he believed that whatever God says was true, he was saved too. And it's like that with us. God doesn't say we're going to have many children or that we need to build a big ark. He says, 'My Son died to pay for all of your sins so you won't have to. And then I raised Him from the dead. Do you believe Me? Do you trust that what I say is true?' Jacobo, all He wants from you is your faith, that you believe Him."

And that's when a light came on in his eyes. He straightened up, smiled and nodded and said, "That makes sense to me. I believe it."

I asked him, "Would you like to tell God what you just told me?" He nodded and repeated after me the prayer at the end of the booklet. "Lord Jesus, I need You. Thank You for dying on the cross for my sins. I open the door of my life and receive You as my Savior and Lord. Thank You for forgiving my sins and giving me eternal life. Take control of the throne of my life. Make me the kind of person You want me to be. Amen."

Jacobo picked his head up, opened his eyes and smiled a huge smile and then stood up and gave me a big gorilla hug.

I was so happy for him, and he was happy for himself too.

"Well, it's getting late. We really should get some sleep," I said.

He agreed and we each lay down on our little beds and turned the lights out. It was nice that he had found Jesus and everything, but I still didn't trust the guy, and I wasn't about to take the chance of waking up to a knife being plunged into my heart and lungs over and over again. So, I laid still and listened. The plan was, as soon as I heard his constant breathing rhythm, Blue and I were going to make like Santa Claus and leave his presence and then come back in the morning. I laid there for at least 15 minutes listening to his breathing and then, all of a sudden, the next thing I saw was a bright light in front of me shining like the sun. And actually, that's what it was. Apparently, I had fallen asleep and when I woke up in the morning, the sun was coming through the window on my face. I had fallen asleep and thankfully, Jacobo had too. I sat up in bed, which made Blue wake up too and shake and that woke Jacobo up. We all sat up together in that little room and looked at each other. It was a little tense.

I invited him to a church that was in the town where he lived and told him we could get going in a few minutes. He kind of agreed, then dipped out a little more cocaine and snorted it up. We talked for a few more minutes, and he said he needed to go do some stuff, but that he'd go to church some other day.

I never saw Jacobo again, but I still pray for him now and then when I think of him. When it was all said and done, I ended up getting 6 free tacos, 3 free beers and a good story out of it all.

Selling Leather
the Hard Way

By April of 2002, I was in a funk and not comfortable with the fact that Juan Diablo wanted me dead. Real estate in Mexico was still in the crapper. I was almost out of money. I had eaten up all of the taco credit at the taco stand. And I didn't know what to do next. Should I go get a real job, or should I try to get more money together to get those leather bags that were waiting for me in Leon?

Blue and I drove up to the peak of a friend's mountain and camped for a couple of days with just some water, a hammock, my Bible and some dog food for Blue. I don't do it very often, but fasting always helps to clear my mind and gets me praying. When I fast, I determine ahead of time what I'm hungering for from God. Then, when I feel hunger, I pray, "God, I hunger for Your direction or wisdom or resolution or whatever it is I determined ahead of time. This time, I went hungry and prayed and read my Bible a lot, and after a couple of days I clearly felt that I should go back to the US and get this leather business going once and for all.

I had enough gas money to get up to my sister's house in Fort Worth, but not much further. When I got there, I got a job as a physician headhunter, cold calling physicians to see if they wanted to move to a different hospital. I didn't really like it, but I got more doctors to sign up in 2 weeks than anyone else had. But after 2 weeks, they fired me because they said that they didn't expect me to be there long since I was always talking about Mexico and they needed someone to commit to a longer time. They also said that I "wasn't professional enough," whatever that means. I got paid for two weeks of work and so had plenty of money now to get home to Portland and eat well on the way.

On June 21st of 2002, the longest day of the year and the first day of summer, I turned 31 and was still just trying to figure it all out. I was single, didn't have a job and didn't really know what the future held, but I knew this. I was on a mission to get this business going come Hell or high water.

In July, Blue and I jumped into the old faithful and headed to Portland again. After all these years out and about, I was living with my parents again, but I wasn't in the basement and I had a plan. My plan was to save money like crazy for one year to get enough money to buy those 5 bags that were still (hopefully) sitting there in Don David's workshop. I decided that, at the end of one year, if I hadn't saved enough money, then I would sell my beloved Land Cruiser and use that money to get things started.

By day, I worked as a maintenance guy for my sister, painting apartments, fixing leaky pipes and unclogging toilets, and by night, I edited my dad's devotional commentary on the book of Revelation, *Strange Work*. It is honestly the best and easiest to understand book I've ever read on what the Bible says will happen at the end of the world. And he wrote it for the everyman to read, not just for theologians.

·

SELLING MY FRIEND

In June of the next year, I gathered all the money I had saved: $157. While I'd made some great memories that year, I didn't have a great savings plan, so it was on to Plan B. I had to sell the Land Cruiser, and it made me sick. We had become friends over the years and had been through a lot together. I loved my Iron Pig as much as a man can love a vehicle, but a man does what a man has to do.

I had no idea what it was worth, but I knew it would go for a decent amount since I always got so many compliments on it. I got some nice pics of it and wrote a lengthy and fun description about its history around Mexico and the US, and some funny manly stories about owning such a rig, and then listed it on eBay for a 7 day auction. I set the reserve at $7,000 so I wouldn't have to sell it if nobody bid up to that.

Well, 2 days in, I got a message from someone in Georgia asking what the reserve was. When I told him, he kindly asked if I would remove it from eBay and sell it to him. He said he would wire me the money right away. I agreed and took the listing down. Little did I know the storm I had just caused. I immediately got 2 emails, one from a guy in California and one from someone in Utah, saying they would pay $10,000 for it that same day if I would not sell it to the man I'd said yes to. And then the next day, I got a message from a guy in Connecticut who said he'd been planning to bid up to $14,000 for it and asked if I would please put the listing back up. Holy cow!

Up to that point in life, according to the IRS, the most I had made in any one year was $12,400. I really needed the extra money to start the business. So, I called the guy in Georgia to tell him the whole story and kindly asked if he would let me out of it so I could relist it. He kindly said no and asked me to honor my word. It wasn't a hard decision to make, but it was painful. I sold that great old Toyota friend of mine for only $7,000.

Seeing how much money I could have made with my Land Cruiser, I took the money from the sale of the 1971 and bought a 1977 FJ55 in Golden, Colorado, for $3,500 and drove it to Juarez, Mexico, to fix it up. It took about 4 weeks to have it fully reupholstered, painted and the brake cylinders rebuilt. And I put on BF Goodrich All Terrain tires. They looked great, last a really long time, are quiet on the highway and do a great job offroad. When all was said and done, I had a total of $7,000 into the Land Cruiser and sold it on eBay for $12,100.

So this was what it felt like to be rich. I finally had enough money to pay for those other 5 bags that Don David made and get even more bags made. But is that what I did? Hindsight is 20/20, but I'd just about doubled my money in one month so why not do it again? What could possibly go wrong?

It was now August and I found a 1968 Toyota Land Cruiser up in Massachusetts in a town named Athol. But I needed a way to get that Land Cruiser back to Juarez. So, I found a little Toyota pickup for sale in the Boston area, just like the one my dad had, and used it to pull the Land Cruiser back with. It was for sale for $1,500 and only had 155,000 miles on it. It was practically brand new, as far as Toyotas go. It pulled the Land Cruiser all the way back to Juarez at 70 mph like it was pulling the wind.

But when I got to Juarez, I realized the Land Cruiser was going to need a lot of expensive, hard to find parts to get it sellable. I found a pair of rusty FJ40s for sale in Kentucky and bought them for parts. Blue and I jumped back into the little Toyota and drove up there to get them. We pulled the first one back to Juarez and then immediately turned around and went back for the second one. Altogether that month, I drove a little over 13,000 miles, but this time listening to sweet and wonderful music because the pickup had a radio. The rear tire of one of the Land Cruisers came off while driving in the middle of the night and smashed into the windshield of an oncoming pickup truck, but other than that, it went as smoothly as could be expected.

THE 18 MONTH PAINT JOB

That's when I learned another lesson. With my eyes big and excitement on my face, I told the pastor who'd painted the last Land Cruiser, "Dude, guess how much I sold the Land Cruiser for? $12,100. Can you believe it?"

He said he was really happy for me, but his words didn't seem to match up with his face. I could tell it bothered him that he did all the work, and I made all the money.

When I pulled those old Land Cruisers to the poor pastor's house and asked him to get started on the next one, his price almost doubled from $1,000 to $1,800. I didn't have a choice, didn't have much money and that price would leave me with just a couple thousand dollars left. It's a good thing he said he would get it done in just a month.

I had found a high quality, really busy autobody shop that said they could have the Land Cruiser fully restored with the best paint job in town in 4 weeks, but they wanted $2,400 to do it. So, I went with the pastor working out of his garage to save a buck. I was penny wise but dollar foolish. Most of the best lessons learned are not learned through good times but through the dumb ones.

The Chinese have a saying, "Trust your friend, but tie up your horse," and I hadn't learned that one yet either. The man of God asked for the full $1,800 in advance, and I naively gave it to him. In case you're young and naive and you haven't been screwed this way before, you *never never never* give all of the money up front for any job. You give it out as you see progress. You can start with enough money for the cost of materials or maybe like 35% down, but then drip the rest out and then pay the last 25% after you have inspected it.

For the next 18 months, I would show up at the pastor's house and hang out the whole day because nothing happened to the Land Cruiser unless I was sitting there. He had already spent my money so he could work on the other cars he had sitting around so he could get the final 25 percent payment from them. He had no motivation whatsoever to finish mine.

I should have taken it over to the $2,400 body shop, but I was too cheap. Being cheap is expensive. It was those lessons of buy nice or buy twice; buy the best, cry once. That shaped the marketing of my bags.

I found a little $100 a month apartment in Juarez, Mexico, right across the Rio Grande from El Paso, Texas, to live in while I was getting the Land Cruisers looking and running great. There was no hot water and Blue and I had to sleep on the floor, but I didn't figure we would have to live there too long before I had a lot more money and could move into a nicer place. Once I'd gotten settled in Juarez, Blue and I made the 19 hour white knuckle drive south to Leon to see if Don David still had those 5 leather bags. It had been over 2 years since I'd been there, but I walked into his little shop and said, "*Hola*, Don David! Do you remember me?" He looked at me and his eyes lit up. There was an eruption of greetings and hugs, and I felt like the prodigal son coming home.

Don David sent his son, Mauricio, into the back, not to kill the fatted calf but to get my 5 leather briefcases. I was so relieved and gladly paid the second half of the bill. We talked about how I could get more of these bags made by them without driving down each time. I got their Mexican bank account info so I could make deposits in Juarez, and then Mauricio and I went to El Mercado de la Luz leather market to pick out a few more hides to start my next order. The next day, Blue and I jumped back into our little Toyota pickup and headed north.

Over the next few years, I asked many questions and learned all I could about leather and quality and construction from my new mentor. Don David patiently explained the differences between full grain, top grain, genuine, split and bonded leather. He taught me about the different types of thread we could use and explained why having the right number of stitches per inch was so important when using different thicknesses of thread. It was like going to school all over again, but this time I wasn't learning Greek, I was learning quality and design, and I couldn't get enough.

QUALITY LEATHER

Because I think everyone should know how to choose quality leather, let me summarize what I learned from Don David and what we try to tell our customers one of the reasons why our bags are worth paying more for. If you've ever looked at leather products, you will have seen terms like *full grain leather, top grain leather, genuine leather, split leather, suede* or *bonded leather*. But no one had ever explained each term for me in a simple way that I could understand. So, here's my attempt to explain it.

For example, great leather is like a great roof. It'll keep the water and weather out, protect the inside of the house and last a long time. In the US, we build a roof by laying big thick sheets of plywood on top of the house's frame to serve as the base layer. Then we take big rolls of tar paper or some membrane and cover all of the plywood. That first layer of tar paper isn't super protective, but it will keep the water out. But we need more long term protection and durability, so we lay down a super tough, dense and protective layer of shingles on top of the tar paper that sits on top of the thick bottom layer of plywood. The top layer protects from water and hail and all kinds of junk for many, many years. The plywood, tar paper and shingles all together make up the roof, but it's the tough shingle layer that makes up the top 25 percent of the roof that is the most protective and most important.

Leather initially comes about as thick as a smartphone and, like a roof, has different layers. The bottom 75 percent of the leather is called the *corium* and it's like the plywood on a roof. The top 25 percent is called the *grain*. It's like the tar paper and shingles, and it's where the toughest and most tightly woven fibers are. The fibers are so tight that water and things that leave stains have a tough time penetrating, and the moisture inside the leather has a tough time getting out to dry the leather.

The grain layer is way denser and more protective than the rest of the leather, and it's what gives leather its reputation for toughness. If you evenly split the top half of the hide from the bottom half of the hide, the top half will weigh more than the bottom half.

But not many people want leather purses and jackets as thick as a smartphone, so they make the hide thinner by one of two ways.

The first way is by splitting off the top half of the hide from the bottom half and now there are 2 hides. The top half of the hide still has the *FULL* amount of *grain* on it, and so they call it *full grain leather*. The bottom half of the hide doesn't have any grain on it, and so they call it *split leather* and it's really inexpensive to buy. Confusingly, it can technically be called *genuine leather* or *suede* too. The makers of knock off and low quality bags press and paint the split leather to try to make it look like natural full grain leather, but it's not nearly as strong or protective. It dries out and cracks sooner, and water and stains soak in more easily. And since the fibers aren't as tightly woven together, the fibers let go of their grip of each other and pull apart sooner and tear.

The second method for making a hide thinner is by shaving or sanding off the top 15 to 20 percent of the hide to get rid of that unsightly marbling and what some people consider the icky and ugly natural markings of the cow. Those scars come from barbed wire and mesquite trees or bites from bugs, bats or coyotes, but get sanded off and most of the grain with it. If it still has some of the grain left on the *TOP*, they call it *Top Grain leather*. That means they don't have to cut around the imperfections in the whole hide and throw those pieces away. Since leather is really expensive, they can now use up more of the hide and save a ton of money. What they do now is paint it a flat color and *presto*, it looks like vinyl. Or they stain it and distress it so unsuspecting people think it's great *Full Grain leather*, but really it's just pretty good *Top Grain leather*, like a roof that has tar paper but no shingles. When someone is manufacturing 100,000 bags and they're saving $20 of leather per bag, you do the math.

Imagine someone tried to sell you a basic plywood roof that had shingle print on it but didn't have any tough and protective tar paper or shingles. *That would be like Genuine, Split or Suede leather. Bonded leather* would be the equivalent of sheets of pressed and dried dog poop glued to the frame of your house where plywood would normally be. Early on, I committed to only using the toughest leather I could get my hands on (*Full Grain*), and then we use the thick version of it.

GOING CRAZY FOR THEM

I drove over to my sister's house in Texas to sell the 5 bags on eBay. It was like going on vacation when I went there. They had hot water and Jeanne was a good cook. Plus, I'd only ever sold my Land Cruiser on eBay, so she helped me understand the ins and outs of how to list the bags right.

The first bag description I'd ever written was just one big paragraph. But this time, I wrote about what I'd learned about quality, how I'd redesigned the bags, as well as some stories about my adventures with Blue and about Don David's input and why these bags were built for the long haul. I listed all 5 bags at once for a 7 day auction and sat back to watch.

The people went crazy. I got so many questions but even more compliments. One guy wrote, "Nice bags. I love the stories. Give Blue a scratch behind the ears for me . . . if there is a 'Blue.'" A lot of people thought I had made it all up.

We had no idea how much the bags would sell for. The one we'd sold a couple years back went for $335, but we were selling 5 this time. In retrospect, I should have sold them one at a time, because I didn't know that when you list multiple bags on the same listing, everyone only has to pay what the lowest bidder bids.

When the auction ended, the fifth highest bidder came in at $355. Nobody could believe it. We jumped around the room high fiving and hugging again, and then we got kind of quiet and looked at each other. Did what just happened, happen?

Quite a few friends and family had told me I was wasting my life pursuing this, that I needed to settle down, get a regular job, buy a house and a minivan and get married and then I would be happy. But this sale was confirmation that I wasn't crazy for doing what I was doing and that I had something I could earn a living with.

More emails came pouring in. They told me sad stories about how they'd either slept through the end of the auction, forgotten about it, gotten outbid at the last second, or some other thing, and asked how they could get one. They wanted to know when I would have more bags and if they could order one in advance without bidding. It's hard to describe the feelings I had and the thoughts that were flooding my head, but let's just say they were really good ones.

GOOD ENOUGH OR GREAT?

Shortly after getting home, I went to the Juarez bus station to pick up the next 4 bags Don David had made, and on October 21st, 2003, I started selling them on eBay regularly. Pete and Dennis were the father and son mechanic team in El Paso, at PDL Enterprises, who used to regularly repair my cursed VW Bus. They said I could use their office and the computer at night for $100 per month. I also used their address to first register Saddleback Leather Co. as an official business in the State of Texas.

That's when I started to think about what kind of company I wanted Saddleback to become. My first bag wasn't too hard to design, and people went crazy for it. But when I decided to make this into an actual business and design more bags, there were 2 roads I could walk. As someone once said, "Good enough is the enemy of great." Did I want to take the fast and easy "good enough" road or the long and hard "great" one?

The "good enough" road was littered with cheap and torn, tear stained leather bags made with zippers, magnets, Velcro, snaps and buttons. They were easy to design and just good enough to get the job done, but the "great" road was another story. It looked like it hadn't been walked much for a couple of generations, but it was lined with long lasting, impressive bags of envy.

I chose to intentionally give myself the constraint of no zippers or breakable parts, and that forced me to innovate and avoid joining the "The Just Good Enough" club. The last thing I wanted was to have my designs blend in with the masses.

Fast forward a few years. This commitment to the "Great Club" meant brutal and time consuming efforts to come up with ways to close bags securely so toothpaste wouldn't fall out of a toiletry kit or underwear wouldn't be visible through the gaps in a duffle bag. Slowly, but surely, we launched more and more bags that stood out from literal boatloads of generic looking, mediocre bags being pumped out one a minute.

Our style was uncommon, and that's what caught people's eye. There hadn't been many old fashioned bags on the market since our grandfather's day. Saddleback's design style was different from pretty much everyone else's, except maybe Louis Vuitton's.

ADDING VALUE

At the beginning, I usually had a bag to sell each week, and they normally sold for north of $600. With that money, I would then buy dog food, pay my rent and cell phone bill and then deposit most of what was left into Don David's Mexican bank account, so they could send more bags up on the bus. I also occasionally sold VW buses and other old cars on eBay for Pete and Dennis, and they paid me $500 per vehicle.

Now that I was settled and making plenty of money, I got back to what I wanted to do all along; work with youth. On Halloween night of 2003, I met a man at church named Joe Bahr, who was the Young Life director in that region, and I started playing guitar and speaking at the El Paso Young Life Club under him. Joe was a big part of my life, as a mentor, for those 3 years in Juarez.

Since the leather briefcases were so photogenic, I started taking pictures of them in cool places around Texas, Oregon, the Rocky Mountains, Mexico and anywhere else I drove to. One time in Morelia, I stopped a *federale* and asked him to pose with the briefcase and his AK-47. And he did. I also got a few great shots of Blue with the bag. All of the pictures backed up the stories, and I think some of them made people smile.

I added surprise gifts in a lot of the bags that people bought. Once I bought about 50 red friendship bracelets from a little boy in downtown Juarez and tied them onto the front belt loops of each bag. I didn't live far from a coffee roaster in Juarez, so I often bought a half kilo of fresh roasted coffee beans to send with the bags. I just wanted to make the new owner smile, and I knew I would like it if someone did that for me.

If you're wanting to improve your business, add more value to what you're selling than your competitors do. Try just helping people out in life and make them smile, even if it costs you a little more. I bet your customers will appreciate it.

PLANNING NOT TO EAT

By June of 2004, the Land Cruiser was still only 25 percent done. All of the $12,100 I had from selling the FJ55 was long gone. This wasn't how it was supposed to go. Don David wasn't always as excited about making my bags as he was about making belts for the little boys of his lifelong clients and I think he was right to make the choices he did.

But that led to one time I didn't have any bags to sell and none on the horizon for 2 more weeks. Then, it would be another week before the auction would end so I could get paid. I had $19 in my bank account, a full tank of gas and a new bag of dog food and that's it.

It's amazing how our prayer life gets strong in hard times. So, I prayed and prayed for God to pull me through and a peace came over me when I realized I wasn't going to die. I would just drink water and fast and use this lean time to focus more on prayer. It's not like I would be making my dog fast too. And it was just 3 weeks of not eating.

About 2 days later I got a call from a strange number. "Hello, Mr. Munson? Where would you like your insurance check sent?"

I sat there for a few seconds in silence and then asked, "What are you talking about?"

The man on the phone reminded me that well over a year ago, I'd been rear ended while waiting at a traffic light, and the insurance company had a $1,900 check with my name on it and just needed an address to send it to. The next day, Pete and Dennis at PDL asked if I could sell a 1962 Porsche 356 for one of their clients and another VW bus that had just come in. I ended up making $3,200 that month, which was more money than I had ever made in any one month of my life, minus selling the Land Cruisers. Go figure.

THE SUITCASE

At about that time, a business consultant customer of mine wrote in to give me some advice. He said, "I've been in the consulting world for the past 25 years, and I don't know why I'm giving you this free advice, but I feel compelled to."

He said that I had a very cool thing going and that this was the way things were going to go down if I kept going: I would keep selling the bags, and they would grow in popularity, and then when people started to take notice, others would copy my bags and sell them for cheaper. I would then go out of business because I was just one more guy selling a leather bag like everybody else's, but at a higher price. Instead, what I needed to do was develop the brand to become more well known and diversify the product line to offer more than just a single bag.

I took his advice to heart. My mind thought back to my old suitcase. One thing I'd always wanted was an old leather suitcase. Back in 1990, my Great Aunt Lelia Jane Collins offered to pay for my college if I would go to New Mexico State University. So, I told my parents I was leaving Portland State University to go there. Lo and behold, it was the perfect time for my parents to move from Oregon and get back to New Mexico too. Dad had a great childhood growing up hunting and fishing in Truth or Consequences, New Mexico, and he wanted that for my 7 year old little brother too. So, we all moved together in February of 1990.

We poured all of our earthly belongings into a big 5' x 10' trailer and my mom, dad and brother pulled it behind their Plymouth Volare station wagon at 45 mph from Oregon to New Mexico. I followed behind in my first car, a 1981 Pontiac Phoenix Hatchback. When we got to T or C, Dad got a job as the night clerk at Best Western by the highway and somehow figured out how to buy an old, run down, thick walled adobe house for $19,000. It wasn't pretty, but it was ours.

But the house included a hidden treasure. When I opened the detached garage, I found an old fashioned, brown leather suitcase all dried out and kind of torn up. It looked so cool. Now, *that* was a suitcase Indiana Jones would use.

That suitcase was dear to me. It was one of the only things I had in that faith testing time. And so I asked Don David to make me a suitcase like it. The one he made me turned out even cooler than the one I used to have. It looked like I was going into the luggage business.

BUSINESS BROTHERS

I was selling a bag almost every week, but then there wouldn't be deliveries for a month or two, so I would call and plead and Don David would finally send a few more. But then the deliveries would stop again. Money was obviously not the main driver for Don David. It was the relationships that came with the work.

I learned that every 3 months or so, Blue and I needed to hop into that little faithful Toyota pickup and white knuckle it down to Don David's shop to pour into the relationship. That same 5 gallon bucket was always there for me to turn over, put a pad on top of and sit down to chew the fat with him. I'd usually go get him a water and we'd talk as he worked. I learned a lot about quality and leather, but Don David taught me a lot about life too. When the relationship was right, the leather bags would flow to the north. When the river would slow, we would drive back down.

In October I was telling my little brother, Jonathan, that I was going to focus on selling more bags so I could get the Land Cruiser finished up. He was in the Marines at the time, living in Tunisia, North Africa, guarding the American embassy, but had been saving a ton of money there, and so out of the blue, he offered to loan me a little money to get the Land Cruiser unstuck.

I agreed and told him, "Thank you, brother. You loan me the money and I'll double it."

He knew all about the leather bags and had seen firsthand how excited everybody was about them. About a week later, I had $6,000 deposited in my account.

The day after the money was in the bank, I started looking for a new autobody guy. I visited the really busy paint shop again, but their price was still $2,400. I was still too cheap, so I kept looking for a better deal because I still didn't understand the whole idea of cash flow.

I found a new body guy, Pedro, who I talked down to $1,100. I was so proud of myself. I marched over to the pastor and pulled the original FJ40 and the other 2 Land Cruisers over to Pedro. Little did I know, Pedro struggled to work consistently because he was drunk all the time. But about 6 months later and 80 hours of me sitting on an overturned 5 gallon bucket to force him to work on it, it was finally painted. In the meantime, I borrowed another $4,000 from Jonathan to get by.

It's not the easy and fun times that shape us into who we are, it's the hard and humbling ones that do. Looking back now, I wouldn't have wanted it any other way. Being stuck in Juarez, being taken advantage of and learning lessons the hard way all shaped me into the man I am today and is part of what made Saddleback Leather into, well, Saddleback Leather.

Pedro finished in April of 2005, and I now owned a blue, fully restored FJ40 Toyota Land Cruiser. I took some cool pictures, wrote some fun, exciting stories and sold it for $18,000 on eBay. Right away, I asked Jonathan if he wanted to reinvest his $10,000 so I could buy 50 more bags. He said, "Absolutely!"

Having my brother to talk to through this with was so refreshing. I didn't really have anyone else. I figured he would make a great co-owner of this leather company. So, I offered him 50 percent of the business, but he hesitated and said he would get back to me. And when he did, he thanked me for the kind offer but said that he'd been accepted into Wheaton College and didn't want to be obligated to work at his big brother's leather business when he graduated. So, he kindly declined.

In May of 2005, I found a brown 1979 FJ40 in great shape in northern New Mexico that I brought back to Pedro to paint yellow with black accents. He finished it in only 2 months because I didn't pay him all at once. I also sold that one for $18,000 and paid Jonathan $20,000, double his $10,000 investment, since he didn't want to buy into the business.

THE SADDLEBACK LEATHER NAME

By August, it was time to formalize all of this into a business. I was making more money than I'd ever made in all my life, and it was obvious it was turning into something significant. Now I just needed to give it a name.

Up until that point, none of my bags had any kind of distinguishing mark on them, and I liked it that way. Maybe I could call it "Unbranded" or "Unmarked," and it would be the anti-brand leather company. If you needed a name brand to help you feel like people would finally respect you, then this was not the bag for you. That was one idea.

My grandfather's name was Jack Barbour, and I always thought he had a good, strong sounding name. And that past Christmas, Jonathan had given me a CamelBak backpack to drink from when I was riding my mountain bike. So, I thought putting "back" on the end of any word gave it a good, strong sound. Hmm . . . what other words or names had "back" on the end? There was a mountain overlooking Truth or Consequences called Turtleback. That was a cool name. Turtleback Leather?

I was getting somewhere now. Turtleback, CamelBak and Leatherback all had a good sound to them. Then there was Saddleback Mountain outside of Portland, Oregon, which was a good place to hike. Turns out, any mountain that has 2 peaks with a dip in between is called a "saddleback" mountain. Megachurch pastor Rick Warren named his church Saddleback because of the Saddleback Mountain in their area.

I was discussing it with Dad, and he really liked the name Saddleback Leather. I preferred Turtleback or Leatherback more, but he kept telling me about how with having the word *saddle* in the name it described the thick and tough nature of the designs. He had a point. But I didn't want to be boxed in to a cowboy brand. *Saddleback* in the name would force me to fight the branding battle with everyone saying "Yeeeehaaaaw!" and "Giddy up, partner!" in their minds every time they thought of the company. Even though I like a lot about the cowboy culture, I would have to work hard for people to understand that we were Clint Eastwood meets Indiana Jones, not John Wayne meets Garth Brooks.

When I asked my brother his opinion, he reminded me that there were a lot of companies with dumb names that were successful. Like Gucci, for example. Or the brand Coach. What dumb sounding names for fashion brands. He said my company was going to be successful, regardless of the name, and he was right.

So, Saddleback Leather Co. was the name I registered with the State of Texas and officially opened the business.

THE FIRST BIG "MARKETING" TRIP

In September of 2005, I wanted to wander on a 6 week trip through Eastern Europe to look around and to North Africa, to visit Jonathan. I asked Mom if she would watch Blue and asked Dad if he would list a bag on eBay each week and ship it out while I was gone. They both agreed.

I jumped onto an airplane bound for Frankfurt, Germany, with my fairly empty leather suitcase, a full briefcase with a colorful Mexican serape blanket strapped onto the top and a 2 megapixel Sony point and shoot camera. My plan was to not have a plan. I knew I had a specific date to catch a flight from Munich to Tunisia to visit my brother, and I had to be back in Frankfurt in 6 weeks for the return flight back to Oregon, but other than that, there was no plan, which made the trip even more fun.

Arriving in Frankfurt, I made my way to the train station. I knew I wanted to go to Eastern Europe because it was less crowded and much cheaper. At the train, I checked the schedules on the board and one of the next trains was going to Prague, Czech Republic. That sounded good.

Several hours later, I picked up my leather suitcase and satchel and stepped off the train in the most beautiful city I had ever seen. It was so cool it almost looked fake.

It was in Prague where my routine of product photography was established for years to come. I went straight to the nearest postcard rack and bought the ones I thought would look nice with a leather bag and suitcase in them. I then showed the cards to locals and asked them how to get there. I spent the first 2 days wandering from site to site, planning the best place to take the pictures from, based on the time of day, and then got some really great shots that we still use today.

After I got some great pics in Prague, I headed to Krakow, Poland, which was beautiful in every way you can imagine. From there, I stopped in Budapest, Slovenia, and then went on to Salzburg, Austria. From Austria, I made it over to Munich, Germany, to experience the home of Oktoberfest and catch my flight down to see my brother in Tunisia, North Africa. We wandered around that beautiful desert country, and I got a ton more shots of the suitcase and briefcase.

BACK TO JUAREZ WITH TREASURES

I knew my dad was intelligent and entrepreneurial and he always had a lot of ideas of how to make things better. But I was about to learn how gifted his mind really was. Little did I know, my dad was really good at tracking numbers, analyzing them and then making a business more efficient by making slight changes.

Up until that point, I was strictly selling one leather briefcase each week. Dad took it up a notch while I was gone. Without my permission, he started experimenting to see how many more he could sell without the price going down. He started selling 2 bags at a time for a week. Then one bag at a time on 3 day auctions. And on and on he kept experimenting. The result? Sales doubled while I was gone.

I got back to Juarez in October with a treasure trove of photos to show and stories to write about. The photos I'd taken made Saddleback Leather look more pro than the one man show it was. YouTube had just started, but it hadn't even entered my head to post videos anywhere. Myspace was all there was to social media. I posted some of the pics there, but the rest of this great content I shared with the world via my eBay listings and, later, on our website.

An interesting thing started to happen. Customers started taking pictures of their own bags and sending them in to show off their photography skills too. This gave me the idea of doing a photo contest twice a year with multiple winners in each category. For our last 2024 contest, we received about 650 entries. A lot of people had a lot of fun taking those pictures, and a lot more people had a lot of fun looking at them.

I can easily see now what was driving the company's success. It was our customers. I had friendships with them and was talking with them and emailing them back even when I didn't have to. I would even check in on them to see how they were doing. When they would lose an eBay auction, I knew them and would send them messages like, "That one was close. Keep trying. You'll own one, one day." It was so fun building rapport with all of these people and keeping in touch.

Today, we only hire people in customer service who love making friends with people. They chat with our customers and really get to know who they are. I tell my team, "If time allows, spend a little extra time on the phone to find out about who is calling." Sometimes our people will hear about something sad going on in our customers' lives and ask if they can pray for them right then and there. Later, they'll call or email them back to see how they're doing. Maybe we're doing it all wrong, but if we're going to err, we're going to err on the side of relationships.

SADDLEBACKLEATHER.COM

In December of 2005, my friend Roman finished our first website, and it went live. I couldn't believe that Saddlebackleather.com was formally a thing. I didn't do much with it to start, but it was just cool to have. It was still amateur hour and the site didn't perform all that great, but that didn't matter. I had a website!

In January of 2006, I asked Dad if he wouldn't mind posting some more of my bags on eBay while I went on another trip with Jonathan now that he was out of the Marines. He agreed and kept up the analyzing and testing. Jonathan, Uncle Pat and I flew down to Costa Rica and Panama to surf a little and get some more pics of my bag and suitcase. It was quite the trip and I didn't wear a shirt one time.

I was at an internet cafe on one of the Bocas Del Toro islands and saw 2 things that made my eyes bulge. First, I checked eBay to see how the bags were selling, and saw that Dad had just sold 2 bags for $710 *each* on a 3 day auction! And, Dad reached out to the third highest bidder, who lost the auction and had bid $705, with a second chance offer for $705. He took it. That means we sold $2,125 worth of leather bags in a 3 day period. Apparently, there was more demand for my bags than I realized, which was a beautiful thing.

Family to the Rescue

Selling those bags was not nearly as eye popping as the next thing I saw. After eBay, I went on to check Myspace and that's when my whole life changed. I looked and there was a message from a really pretty girl named Suzette, asking me, "Where is Multnomah Bible College?"

I checked her out, and let's just say I was definitely attracted. She was wearing a slightly cutoff shirt that showed her belly button and a little tattoo of Tigger sticking up partially above her jeans. I started going through her Myspace profile, and she was talking about how much she loved God and how important her personal relationship with Him was to her. All great, so far. But then I saw a picture of her gutting a deer. That was when I *knew* that she was the one for me. No bathing suit or lingerie shot could have made her more attractive than seeing her leaning over that dead deer with a bloody knife in her hand. As a bonus, I found out she did bookkeeping for a living. Are you kidding me? A hot and sexy, godly *bookkeeper* who can gut a deer? I just knew that I knew it was meant to be.

In February of 2006, I hired Dad (the rest of the world calls him Herb Munson) full time to help me with the business. He had been a pastor for so many years, but God had moved him on to other things, which turns out, was Saddleback Leather. Up until then it was all me, and I needed help. Since Dad had quadrupled our sales, I could now afford him.

TEXAS, HERE I COME

By February 2006, I had lived for 2½ years in the most dangerous city in the world, and I'd had enough. I was tired of wondering if my truck would be there in the morning and having to leave the glove box open at night so my loving neighbors wouldn't break the window only to find that I wasn't hiding anything in there. I was tired of the drug dealers and prostitutes on the corner and the same foot cop always trying to pull me over for a bribe at that 5-way intersection by the house. I always acted like I didn't see him running toward me or hear him yelling for me to pull over as he chased me on foot.

In February of 2006, my dad suggested maybe it was time for me to move out of that Juarez hell hole and buy a house in El Paso. I had $40,000 in the bank for a down payment, so it made sense. My credit wasn't all that great, but I found a house for sale by owner and talked the wonderful Halloul family into selling it to me on a contract. About 4 days later, I was the proud owner of my first home.

I've heard it said, "A woman will marry the first man she falls in love with, and a man will marry the first woman he falls in love with *when* he's ready to get married." That maxim was certainly true of me, and I was ready.

Suzette and I started talking on the phone when I got back to the US, and when I bought the house, she walked me through buying my first bed. She said that if I was going to use the bed for a third of my life, then I should buy something nice. So, I bought a $1,700 king sized mattress and box spring set that was on sale for $1,100, and Suzette was right. We still use that same bed today 19 years later. Quality remains long after price is forgotten.

Since it was coming up on Valentine's Day, I put a little package together full of heart shaped knickknacks and candies and sent it to her in San Antonio. Since I was an unemployed, 34 year old single man living in Juarez and selling stuff on the internet, she didn't quite trust me yet, so she gave me her work address to send it to. Her family didn't trust me either. Suzette's eldest sister thought for sure I was a serial killer. And honestly, I could see why she might think that.

On February 17th, I left Blue with friends in El Paso and flew to San Antonio to meet Suzette. She picked me up at the airport, and she looked even more beautiful in person. We went straight to her home, where her roommate, Abby, was waiting to meet me too. Within a few hours of landing, we were clothes shopping. Suzette felt it would be best if I dressed better, so I spent $400 on clothes. That was more than I'd spent on clothes in the last 10 years combined, but I thought it would impress her if I could drop that kind of dough without even blinking. On the inside, though, I was dying.

That night, she had friends over to play games as a sort of informal group interview. Remember, love is blind, but your friends and family are not. It worked out pretty well. And by about 3 p.m. the next day, the conversation seriously dropped off and we became an "unofficial" thing, if you know what I mean.

I flew back home and by the next weekend, I couldn't get back to her fast enough. In fact, I got there so fast, I got a speeding ticket along the way. But this time I brought Blue.

I'd been bragging to Suzette about how well behaved and obedient Blue was and how "stay" was his thing. I knew she would be impressed. But as I drove up, she had me pull my little pickup into her garage and I let Blue out there. It wasn't 5 seconds before Blue smelled the neighbor's bitches, who were both in heat at the same time. His eyes widened and he bolted through the open door to the backyard.

And without even slowing down, he hopped over the neighbor's fence, like a deer hopping over a fallen tree in the forest, and immediately started humping the first one he got close to.

Frantically, Suzette yelled out loud, "Hey, get control of your dog!" and, "Oh no! He's going to get my neighbor's dog pregnant!" I was shouting and commanding Blue to come back with the most stern and dominant alpha male voice I could muster. But it was like he had turned his ears off. He was focused on one thing and one thing only.

So, I jumped the fence and grabbed ahold of Blue and threw him back over, but as soon as I jumped back over, he leapt right back over the same fence and started humping again. Suzette was still screaming as I jumped back over and dragged my whining dog into the house. For the entire weekend, Blue hung out by the back window, whining. Love was definitely in the air around Suzette's house for Blue and I both. And it was the last time Suzette allowed me to park in her garage since the 10 year old Extra Cab Nissan pickup I had just bought left a nice pool of oil on her spotless concrete garage floor. I put 70,000 miles on my little Toyota pickup and sold it for more than I bought it for because I needed something with more space for a Mexico roadtrip with my dad and Blue together. But I sold the Nissan just after that and upgraded to a 2001 Toyota Tacoma.

THE PROPHECY

On March 10th, it was Suzette's turn to visit me. So, she bought a one-way ticket to El Paso to see my world for a few days. She flew in Friday and I took her to my singles church group to show her off at game night. The next morning, I picked her up early from Paul and Janette Cook's home, an older couple from my church who had said she could stay with them. As I was waiting for her to get ready, they both pulled me aside and excitedly said, "Oh my goodness, Dave. Suzette is such a wonderful woman. Do whatever you need to do to keep her."

We were headed over to visit a Juarez saddlemaker named Samuel, who had made about 20 briefcases for me as backups for when Don David got tired of making them. If you find one, you can recognize it because they were all unevenly handsewn and had no name or other distinguishing marks on them.

I thought it would be fun for Suzette to see Samuel's place and design a women's belt for him to make. So, Suzette and I stopped by Tandy Leather Factory for her to pick out the natural leather, stain, buckle, studs and other supplies she would need for her first design and then headed across the Rio Grande into Juarez.

About 10 minutes before crossing into Mexico, Suzette's dad, Jerry, called, and I could hear his voice as she talked with him on the phone. He said they'd seen the picture she'd sent of me, and it took forever to load on their dial-up internet connection. He said the picture had revealed me slowly, from my chin up, and when it got to my eyes, they made their call. Jerry said to Suzette, "We saw he has kind eyes. He's the one."

Suzette couldn't believe her dad had just said that, and she knew I'd heard it too. She reprimanded him and then squirmed in her seat before handing me the phone when Jerry asked to speak with me. After greeting each other, he bluntly said, "You're the one who's going to marry my daughter. I just know it."

Suzette could also hear his voice, and you should have seen her face. It was so funny. When she gets embarrassed or uncomfortable, her neck and cheeks get blotchy red. And boy, was she blotchy red then. She grabbed the phone away from me and said, "Dad, I can't believe you just said that! What is wrong with you? Why in the world would you say something like that? That is so embarrassing!" I laughed and laughed and could tell I was going to get along with that guy just fine.

When we arrived in Juarez, I knocked for a while on the door before Samuel's sleepy eyed dad opened up. He was just wearing shorts, but for a man who was 5' 8" and 300 pounds, he had an impressively firm physique. He pointed us toward Samuel's workshop in the back of the house and then laid back down on his bed in the living room. The house was long and narrow, which made us walk through every messy room in their house to get to the back. And when we stepped into the outdoor space between the house and Samuel's workshop, the chickens scattered.

Since it was Suzette's first design, we walked her through it slowly. She seemed to get it. We used the wide belt around her hips to model it after and watched Samuel expertly cut the leather. After it was painted, she could see where she wanted the holes and studs, and that was it for the day. I would pick it up a few days later and bring it to San Antonio that next weekend.

For lunch, I took her to my favorite burrito stand, Burritos Del Oro. As Suzette was finishing her big burrito and licking her fingers, I asked, "Would you like another *horse* burrito?"

"What?" she said, staring at me. "Did you say *horse*?"

I nodded, as if it were nothing, and kept eating my burrito.

She gave me a sly look and said, "You're kidding, right? These aren't made of horse meat, are they?"

I smiled and told her the truth. "Yes, the meat in your burrito is horse. Who knew horse tasted that good, right? Would you like another?"

She didn't think it was that funny and said neigh, she would pass on having another.

LEAVING AND COMMITTING

On March 19th, I was sitting in Suzette's living room waiting for her to get ready when my brother called. He asked about how our relationship was going and if maybe she was the one.

I whispered into the phone, "No, we've been talking about it and I've asked her to be my official girlfriend, but she won't commit to a formal relationship after a month of secretly dating. She had her last boyfriend for 8 years, and I'm not going to wait around for a year or two just to find out she doesn't want to commit. So, I won't be coming back to San Antonio again."

What I didn't realize was, Suzette had overheard the entire phone conversation from the bathroom.

Surprisingly, later that night, Suzette leaned over and quietly said, "Dave, I want to commit to you. I want to officially be your girlfriend."

I couldn't believe my ears. We talked about it for a bit.

Then she said, "So if this turns out to be more serious, about when are you thinking we would get married?"

I thought for a few seconds and said, "Summer, maybe June."

She said, "Oh, okay, June. That would give me a little over a year to plan. That would work."

I turned to her and said, "I was thinking like in 3 months. You mean you're okay with waiting for over a year for sex? Because I'm still waiting until I get married."

That next weekend, we put down the deposit on the wedding venue.

On April 19th, we flew up to Michigan so I could ask her father's permission to marry his daughter. After a little bit of chit chat, he says to me, "Well, you've got to know something about Suzette. She's a tough one. She's the kind of woman who'll push you down on the floor and sit on you." To which I responded, "Well, that's kind of what I was hoping for." He laughed out loud and said, "Okay, you'll do just fine. You can marry my daughter."

On April 24th, Suzette and I went out to eat at Paesanos in San Antonio, and after dinner I asked her to excuse me for a moment. I went straight to the hostess, paid the bill and handed her an envelope to give to Suzette in 10 minutes.

My brother was waiting outside and drove me to the old picturesque church where we were going to get married. I had gotten the key earlier in the day to set it all up, so all I had to do was light the candles that were floating in little jars of water along the walkway leading up to the door and along both sides of the aisle. I then laid a dozen white long-stemmed roses from the door to the altar and spread hundreds of rose petals everywhere in between.

At the restaurant, Suzette opened the envelope and inside were 3 keys and a clue in the form of a poem telling her where to use the next key. The first poem and key were clues to her car. The second poem was the clue to the front door of the chapel with the key to open it. And the third poem led her to the little wooden chest on the altar with the key to open that too.

Let's just say it was pretty darn romantic. When I heard her opening the door to the church, I hid in the dark behind the huge drapes of the altar and watched as she slowly walked up the candlelit aisle. As soon as she read the note inside the chest telling her why I wanted to marry her, I stepped out from behind the curtain and knelt down to ask for her hand in marriage. I told her all that I appreciated and loved about her and all of that mushy stuff that goes along with proposals, and then opened up the little box from my pocket with her ring in it. I opened it and asked, "Will you marry me?"

She said, "Yes."

I couldn't move to San Antonio fast enough. After only 2 months in my new home in El Paso, I rented an apartment about a mile away from Suzette and waited for our wedding date, August 26th, to come.

On May 11th, Suzette and I flew to Portland to introduce her to the family and spend Mother's Day with my mom. Everyone kept saying to me, "Dave, how in the world did you catch someone like her? She's amazing and beautiful and godly and funny and spunky and everything you could ever want." I just shrugged my shoulders, shook my head and smiled.

I was 34 years old and my sister Debbie had told me a million times that I was being too picky and that my list of things I was looking for in a wife was unrealistic and way too long. She said that was why I was never going to get married. Well, you know what?

With Suzette, I got everything on that detailed list except that she wasn't 5' 8". She is 5' 2". But I got everything else I prayed for and more. Plus, she was a *bookkeeper*!

It turns out that was a clear case of bait and switch. Suzette only had that job because she loved the people she worked with, but she was slow and inaccurate at bookkeeping and hated the actual work. I should have included "enjoys bookkeeping" on my prayer list.

HIRING FAMILY

In May, Dad suggested I hire my sister Debbie to do customer service, since she was so good with words, had a great sense of humor and people liked her. And boy, was he right. Debbie would even sometimes write her customer responses in the form of poems. The word started spreading that we loved our customers *and* we sold excessively high quality bags too.

Now getting enough bags to sell was becoming a problem.

Debbie and her 3 kids moved into my El Paso house and lived there for free as part of her pay, which was great for both of us. She set our customer service standards up sky high, like the way it used to be done in America, and then she raised the standard a little bit higher than that.

I will be the first to admit that hiring family members can be tricky. Not everyone is a good fit. Here's how I test family members. I ask them to help out for no longer than 2 months on a specific "temporary assignment" and give them a specific date for when it will end. Then, when it's over, you'll know if you just dodged a bullet or if you should hire them permanently. It works the same with current employees who you are thinking could work in a different role in the company but you're not quite sure.

A month before we got married, I asked Suzette, "How much vacation do you get each year at that job of yours?"

She proudly said, "I get 2 weeks a year, but next year I start getting 3!"

"Seriously? That's horrible and it's not going to work. I'm usually away from home 3 to 4 *months* a year. You're going to have to quit your job."

Oh, she didn't like that. "Wait a second," she responded. "I'm not going to quit. I love my bosses, the owners and my friends there, and they love me too. In fact, I'm going to retire from there one day."

It was clear she didn't understand what kind of life I led and how being tied to a fixed schedule wouldn't work. I defaulted to kindly asking her to pray about it. That's something Christians say that you can't argue with. But I meant it. I didn't want to force it, but I knew I would be miserable if we were tied down like that. It's the reason I had had 25 other jobs before I started Saddleback Leather.

A couple of days later, Suzette brought it up to her boss, Marsha Shields, and asked for her wisdom. Marsha wisely advised her that she would be happier by quitting than by staying. She came back and told me what Marsha said and that she would quit after the honeymoon.

DON'T GET MARRIED!!!

Five days before the wedding, our premarital counselor at church told us not to get married. Yikes. He thought Suzette didn't fully trust me and that we fought too much. He said it would be way easier, less painful and cheaper to cancel the wedding now than to go through a divorce two years later.

Driving back to Suzette's house, we were in shock. We were like, "Okay, so what do we do with that bomb? Can we at least still be friends?" We loved hanging out with each other; we were always laughing and having fun together.

"What do we do with the honeymoon tickets to Bora Bora, though?" Suzette asked. I told her "I guess I'd have to take my brother since I'd already paid for the tickets." She countered that we could both go and she would take her best friend so we could both still enjoy "the most beautiful island on Earth" together. Boy, this was a real bummer.

I thought we should get a second opinion, so I called my other brother-in-law, Dennis, who had been a professional counselor for 25 years, to ask what he thought about it. He listened and talked with Suzette privately and then with me. After hearing both sides, he said, "Oh, you guys are fine to get married. Suzette, here are some things you need to work on and do and how you need to speak with Dave. Dave, here are some things for you to work on, and things you should say and how you should speak with Suzette. But you two are fine to get married." *Phew!* We were so glad to hear it.

The other counselor was just not that experienced. He later said that he learned a lot from counseling us.

So, on August 26th, 2006, we got married, which is one of the best decisions I ever made. And knowing what I know all these years later, I'd make the exact same decision in a heartbeat. But if I could go back in time, we would have gone to marriage counseling a lot sooner.

Suzette still didn't fully understand what she had just become 50 percent owner of, but she was about to find out. She knew people liked our stuff, but to what magnitude, she had no clue until we took off on the honeymoon. The gal at the airport check in counter went on and on about how much she liked our leather luggage.

In California, we had to recheck our suitcases and, standing in line, Suzette leaned over to me and whispered, "Are you kidding me? Everyone is staring at our luggage."

No one said a thing until I caught someone staring and they said, "Excuse me, but your luggage is absolutely stunning. Where did you get it?"

As soon as he said that, the dam broke and the whole line of people started agreeing with the guy who said it. We also got complimented at the Tahiti airports and by half of the resort staff in Bora

Bora. All of these compliments by people who see hundreds of pieces of luggage each month.

Suzette and I both wanted to take full advantage of being in such a cool place, and also turn our honeymoon into a tax-deductible business trip. So, we took a lot of cool photos and videos and posted them for our tiny group of eBay and Myspace followers to enjoy.

Suzette and I were both certified scuba divers, so I bought a deep sea camera housing for my little 2 megapixel Sony camera and then stuffed my briefcase full of fish guts. We went out past the reef, dove 60 feet down and the sharks went crazy. It probably wasn't the smartest idea, but it made some *great* photos and a cool video of the sharks and other fish swimming all around the briefcase and us. When I posted the photos on our site and on eBay, our customers went berserk. I posted the shark video on a new place called YouTube and they went crazy there too.

The photo of Suzette with a knife strapped to her leg, staring at a 9 foot lemon shark 3 feet in front of her face showing his teeth, was my favorite.

I had always thought I needed to hurry up and work the travel and adventure bug out of my system before I got married, since life would shortly slow down to a grind after the wedding, but boy, was I wrong. I'd had some good times and saw some neat things in my single days, but nothing compared to what was heading our way as a married couple.

VAMANOS TO GUANAJUATO

A week later, we got back from the honeymoon and I proposed to Suzette again. But this time, I proposed we move to Mexico to grow the business. She turned to me and said, "You mean you just want to go to Mexico and hope the business grows? No way!"

So, over the next couple of days, I wrote out how I saw Saddleback Leather in my head, 2 years from then, if everything went the way I hoped. I wrote out why moving to Mexico for 3 months was part of it. I wrote down 2 specific objectives for the trip: First, to find a new reliable supplier, since Don David and his son were not able to keep up with demand. Second, I needed to design and launch new products. I listed all of the new designs I imagined and estimated how many of each we would sell and the dollar value that would come from each. I was totally guessing, but that's what all vision statements are about. It was my best guess.

In 2006, I sold $72,000 worth of leather bags in gross revenue, but if we wanted to grow Saddleback Leather past $45,000 of *net* income per year (gross revenue minus expenses), we had to get a steady supply and grow the product line.

On September 5th, I printed out the plan, hopped on the bed and without a word handed the 2 pages to Suzette. She put her book down and started reading. After about 3 minutes of silence, she turned to me and said, "Okay, let's go."

I flew down to Mexico 2 days later to check out the 2 options for apartments to rent that Suzette had found online in the City of Guanajuato. We picked the coolest choice.

I learned then and there that my wife needed something called a *plan*, which provided her with some level of mental security and stability. She later told me that most women crave the security that comes from a plan. She didn't like the idea of going to Mexico just hoping it would all work out. Hope is a terrible plan. Coming up with a vision of how I saw the business in the future was an important exercise, one that has continued to be invaluable for growing Saddleback into a healthy business today.

My Nissan pickup was getting about 20 miles per quart of oil by then, so I sold it and bought my sister's 2001 Toyota Tacoma so I could have peace of mind taking my new bride to Mexico for so long. We packed up the truck to live in the coolest town on the North American continent, Guanajuato, which was only a forty minute drive to the leather capital of North America, Leon. That's where Don David and his son were making my bags and where we make the bags in our own factory today.

It was a 12 hour drive to Leon from San Antonio, so we left early on September 14th so Suzette could experience El Grito on September 15th and the Mexican Independence Day on September 16th. The first day, we took it easy and stopped at a motel near Matehuala, appropriately called Midway, that I had stopped at a few times before. It was about midway between the US and everywhere else you would want to drive to in Mexico.

We had just gotten settled in for the night when her cell phone rang. It was Suzette's dad at first, and he asked if we were at the Midway hotel yet. We thought it was so funny that he knew where we were (we hadn't told anyone where we were staying), but they themselves had wandered around Mexico quite a bit, and that was the popular stop that just made sense. Next, Suzette's mom got on the phone and blurted out, "I had a dream and in it, you were pregnant."

"Whatever, Mom!" Suzette said.

Life and Death

Our new, quaint little house in Guanajuato had a wooden bathtub and a wooden kitchen sink with a beehive-like fireplace in our bedroom. The ceiling was a brick dome. The doorbell was a literal bell above the door that had a thin rope tied to it that went down to the base of the steps for people to pull to let us know they were there. The courtyard was small but sunny with a table and chairs next to a little waterfall. The house was high up on the side of a little valley, so in the mornings we would look out on the opposing side of the valley covered with lots of colorfully painted homes while listening to a braying burro and crowing roosters somewhere down below. To get into town, we walked down a maze of crooked and narrow cobblestone roads and then through a tunnel that took about 5 minutes to walk through.

Suzette and I have intentionally included a lot of healthy, fun and interesting little investments into our marriage that could qualify us as having a pretty good marriage, which we started right from the beginning, such as getting each other coffee in the morning, giving compliments, taking fun trips, going out to lunch or dinner and collecting memories instead of collecting things. This time in our lives was definitely one of them.

We bonded spiritually too. They say couples who pray together, stay together, and it's generally true. On our honeymoon night, I started reading the whole Bible to her out loud, which took us 8 years to finish. It wasn't a great plan, but our plan was better than no plan at all. On the side, we each read the Bible, but together did something special for us.

In Guanajuato, our daily routine was to walk down the valley and through the tunnel into town and have breakfast at some little cafe on one of the plazas. From there, we'd walk another few minutes to Suzette's language school, which was up a tight, colorful little walkway, and then I would turn around and hike back up to our home. From there, I would hop in the Toyota Tacoma and drive to Leon to look for someone new to make my bags.

Don David and his son, Mauricio, had been doing a fine job making bags, but when I began asking them for a higher volume, they couldn't keep up. I mean, they could, but unfortunately, the quality started dropping. They were trying to go so fast that they started missing things. Doing quality work is hard enough, but when you add quantity, it can become a tougher task than most craftsmen can consistently handle.

I spent weeks wandering the streets of Leon looking for a place that could make more bags, but shop after shop told me the bag was too hard and complicated or that they didn't have beastly sewing machines that could push the needle through all of the layers of our thick leather. After about 3 weeks of being told no, I had a novel thought: Why don't I check the phonebook? Sure enough, there was a leather factory.

The owner was a charming guy with sparkly eyes named . . . let's call him "Hanz." If we'd have been neighbors, we would have hung out all the time, until he started cheating me. His dad was an upright, hardworking Austrian immigrant, and Hanz was hardworking too, but that "upright" trait didn't make the jump from father to son.

At that point, I was still wet behind the ears and trusted everybody. Yes, Leonel had cheated me by substituting orange leather for the bags in Morelia and the pastor in Juarez screwed me over, but I still had no idea about all of the ways one could be cheated and stolen from on a larger scale. I cut my teeth with Hanz. Plus, he was the only option. He was able to ship far more bags at a time than Don David, and that's what we needed. It worked for a time, and we finally had enough bags to sell on a regular basis.

SICK AND SENSITIVE

In early November, Suzette was taking a Mexican food cooking class and surprisingly started getting nauseous. She was also getting motion sickness in the truck and her breasts were getting pleasantly plumper (but sadly sensitive). We looked up these strange symptoms and found a possible diagnosis. Even though it was late at night and raining cats and dogs, we drove to the nearest pharmacy to get a pregnancy test.

We parked across from a little pharmacy on the hill. Suzette jumped on my back to cross the street that had become a river, and we picked out a test. When we got back home, she went right to work. A few minutes later, the test came out positive.

How do I say this without hurting my marriage? On a normal day, Suzette is defined by the word easygoing when I'm driving. She gets motion sickness quickly and feels comfortable letting me know when I'm not driving as smoothly as she would like or if I am not accelerating at a rate that she appreciates. Now if you add morning sickness and bumpy, uneven Mexican roads, then the solution was obvious: I put her on the next plane home to Texas, and I loaded up the Tacoma and drove north.

CROCODILE ATTACK

In late 2005, before Suzette and I met, she and her roommate, Abby, had bought tickets to spend Thanksgiving in Australia one year in advance. Once we were married, we found a seat on that same flight for me. And since we were scuba divers, we had big plans to dive the Great Barrier Reef. Honestly, if Suzette hadn't bought a ticket one year in advance, there's no way we would have gone. In the last 3 months, we had been in Bora Bora and lived two months in Mexico, and now she was pregnant. Can you see why I tell people to just buy a ticket? That's the key to going places and learning new things. Just buy a ticket way in advance and it will force you figure it all out and go.

We spent our first Thanksgiving on the northeast coast of Australia in a city named Cairns. Of course, with Suzette being pregnant, they didn't allow her to dive, but she still wanted to go out on the boat. Bad idea. Morning sickness plus motion sickness does not add up to anything good. The boat trip out to the reef was two hours each way, which made it a rough day for everybody, but way worse for poor Suzette.

Like I did with my other trips, I was on a mission to make this trip into a business trip by taking pictures of our bags and suitcases in interesting settings. A couple of days later, we visited a big crocodile park outside of town. I started looking for a place to set my bag next to a giant croc, but I couldn't find the right place. So, I struck up a conversation with a Tasmanian guy working there, named Brett Mawbey, and told him what I was wanting. He thought for a second, looked to the left and right and said, "Okay, mate, come with me," and we rushed off down a path.

We came to a small tour boat and launched off down some canals deep into the park, out of sight and sound of any visitors or employees. He grabbed my bag, lashed it to a long pole and then started looking for a friendly crocodile. It wasn't long before he found a mostly submerged crocodile watching us. Brett grabbed the pole and softly began tapping the bag on top of the water to lure the 9 foot crocodile over. She slowly started swimming toward us and my adrenaline started flowing.

I had the videotape rolling when she struck the bag and started the tug of war. It was so much action and tons of fun. She was pulling and death rolling on it while Brett was pulling and tugging back. It all lasted about a minute before the croc let go of the bag and we pulled it back into the boat.

We laughed and high fived each other and then examined the bag. Sure enough, when I posted those photos on our site and Saddleback Leather's second video on YouTube, our customers couldn't believe what they were seeing.

CSI

We got back to Texas and started preparing for the baby, and part of that preparation was a different vehicle that had room for our baby's car seat. So, we started car shopping. When I got married and had a child on the way, a ferocious "protect and preserve" gene had surfaced in me. I imagined our family broken down on the side of some dark highway with my beautiful wife and daughter, and a beat up truck full of rowdy, Mad Max, beer guzzling hooligans, with Australian accents, pulling over to "help us out." I was sure my words, "But honey, think of all the money we saved by buying this vehicle instead of that reliable one!" wouldn't go over well.

So, I started my search for just the right Toyota. The Tundra was exactly what we needed because it had 4 doors, Blue could ride in the bed when he was all wet or muddy and we could have the back window rolled down. Since the prices for used Toyota Tundras were barely lower than the cost of a new one, it made sense to buy a brand new 2006 Toyota Tundra. And of course, since I owned a leather company, I ordered it with the leather package.

By March of 2007, Dad had taken over all of the company's administrative tasks I wasn't doing, like bookkeeping, tracking customer information and running eBay, and he and Mom had moved back to their home in Truth or Consequences so he could make weekly runs to El Paso to pick up shipments from Hanz. The leather bags were stacked up in his living room and down the hallway, and every day he was taking bags to the post office to ship to customers. Saddleback wouldn't have been able to operate and sell $250,000 worth of leather that year if it wouldn't have been for him.

But something had to give, because Dad couldn't do it all, and we decided it would be the shipping. It just so happened that my sister Patricia and her husband, Dennis Chamberlain, had been considering a complete startover. They said raising their kids in Oregon was beginning to feel like raising them in an R rated movie theater.

I asked if they'd be interested in moving to Texas to handle all of the receiving, inspecting, conditioning and shipping of my bags. They signed on with us, sold their home, moved to Keller, Texas, just north of Fort Worth, and set up shop in their garage to start receiving the bags. They quickly outgrew that space and began operating out of a small storage unit. That was short lived, too, before they began renting an 8,000 sq. ft. warehouse and hired their really great mailman, Abram Wronko, away from the US government to come in and help start managing things.

As the business grew, Patricia and Dennis started a company called Chamberlain Shipping, Inc. (CSI) and, as usual, went over the top on their quality. I didn't ask them to, but they rubbed down each of the leather bags with some sort of leather oils and conditioners, but Dennis wasn't happy with any of them. They were either cheap synthetics, full of deteriorating detergents or too oily.

He became a man obsessed with leather conditioning and really started digging into what determined quality and how to make it. He put his obsessive-compulsive disorder to good use and over the years developed cosmetic grade formulas for cleaning, conditioning and rejuvenating leather for more than just my bags. Dennis developed one UV protectant conditioner specifically for auto interiors, another for shoes and boots, a different one for furniture and more. Lesson learned again: If you're going to create something, why not aim for being the best in the whole world? Dennis and Patricia named their new product Chamberlain's Leather Milk.

By May, we'd next hired Suzette's warm and charming dad, Jerry. He was in a wheelchair most of the time, so he worked online from home. I'd designed a new bag called "The Pouch," which we now call the EDC Satchel (Every Day Carry), specifically for him and told him it was 100 percent his responsibility, which meant ordering the bags, listing them on eBay, handling customer service, solving problems and shipping them. I thought I was doing him a favor, but he blew us out of the water and paid for himself a hundred times over. Our customers *loved* Jerry and he loved them and just kept building our good name.

WELCOME, SELA

On June 7th, 2007, our little baby girl was born. I know you're doing the math in your head. And yes, she's legit. Walking her out of the hospital, loading her up and taking her home in our still new leathery smelling Tundra was such a great feeling. My, how my life had changed in a year and a half. I went from sleeping on the floor of a dumpy $100 a month Juarez apartment with my dog by my side to sleeping in a king-sized bed with my hot wife by my side in a home that I now owned with a new baby in the carseat behind me.

Suzette and I wanted a beautiful name for our daughter, but like a lot of parents, we wanted it to be a little unique and creative without it being weird. I actually wanted *Pietra*, *Francesca* or *Xochitl* (pronounced *so chill*). Suzette wanted *Zara*, and we couldn't agree. We went through every baby naming list there was and found we liked the sound of *Ella*, but that was a little too common. So, I started going through the alphabet saying, *Bella, Della, Fella, Gella, Hella, Jella* and so on until we got to *Sella*. That was it! Sela Munson would be her name.

But not everything changed. Five weeks later, Sela was on her first of many road trips. In her first year she spent about a quarter of her short life in Mexico, rode on 38 airplanes, in 6 boats and logged at least 15,000 miles in the Tundra. By the time she was 5, Sela had 50 stamps in her passport, including a lot of multiples from Mexico and different African countries, and had learned to be a great little traveler.

That haunting prophetic message from the business consultant in 2005 kept ringing in my mind: "Grow or die." Well, they say the best fertilizer for a farmer is his own shadow, so Sela, Suzette and I hopped into the Tundra, drove down to Leon and rented a house so we could spend time to help our business grow. I would be able to see weeds that needed pulling, tend other areas that needed attention and watch out for problems before they got too big. And it worked. I was able to design more bags, guard our quality and keep the supply of bags flowing.

IN MEMORY OF BLUE

In December of 2007, I noticed Blue had developed a hard cough, but only when he was laying down. I took him to the vet, and the news came back cold and hard. The tests showed he had cancer throughout his body and the tumors in his lungs were causing his cough.

Blue had been my constant and faithful companion, wagging his tail millions of times, and if I would have had one, I would have wagged it too. He'd brought so much joy into my life that I can hardly start to tell you. He was a great listener, never complained and protected me when I needed it. In return, I gave him a cool life. When I was sad, he was quiet. When I was happy, he was too. He knew me almost better than any man or woman could, and I knew him almost better than I knew myself.

Blue's life was far from dull. He was killed and revived, run over by me twice, knew more Spanish than most of my friends, was stolen once and fathered puppies in 7 different cities and probably a few places in between. He swam in 23 states, ate as much people food as he did dog food and slept out with me under the stars hundreds of times. Blue had lived a dog's life.

Blue took his first steps in New Mexico, so I knew that that was where he needed to be laid to rest. And it had to be in the desert, near the Rio Grande, where we had played and squandered away so many days together. And so after Christmas, we headed to my parents' house in Truth or Consequences, New Mexico.

Blue was full of energy and he ate well until the end, but on his last day, he could no longer lay down comfortably. To hold on to him any longer would have only been for me, not for him. I knew our friendship couldn't last forever and I dreaded the day I would have to give him back, but that day had arrived. The one hour drive to the vet was the toughest of my life. I don't even know how I drove there with my eyes so full of tears. Blue sat next to me silently, staring at the highway ahead, just like always.

Blue passed away on January 7th, 2008. The next day I found just the right place to honor such a great friend. Dad and I got into his old Ford Bronco, crossed the Rio Grande at the base of the Caballo Mountains and drove up an old, sandy bluff that I knew could never be built on. It was such a remote and beautiful place with the towering mountains behind, the river below and with a view of the valley ahead. I dug a deep grave, lowered Blue's body and covered him up with a big pile of large rocks. Then I stuck the old, thick wooden cross I'd made into the rocks and said goodbye to my faithful friend. And I cried and cried.

The Bible says animals have a spirit, and it also says that all things will be restored and made new one day. I trust that to mean Blue is happier now in Heaven than he ever was with me. As Cicero so eloquently wrote of the death of a friend, "I am disposed to think, therefore, that in his case, mourning would be a sign of envy rather than of friendship."

I am confident Blue is waiting for me to experience Heaven with him, and he wouldn't want to come back to Earth if he could. Of another friend, Cicero wrote, "I find my happiness so much in the hope that my memory of our friendship will be lasting." It rings so true. It has been many years since Blue died, and I still think of him often. Remembering Blue and our exploits still makes me smile.

To quote Cicero once more: "All I can do is urge onto you to regard friendship as the greatest thing in the world; for there is nothing which so fits in with our nature or is so exactly what we want in prosperity or adversity."

· EIGHT ·

Handing Over the Reins

By January 2008, Saddleback Leather had quintupled its sales. It was running fairly smoothly, but I knew I needed a little more help as we grew, so we hired my sister's friend Susan and then Suzette's old roommate, Jana, to help my sister Debbie with customer service. Both of them are still with us today. Susan has been our customer service manager for many years and Jana our HR manager for a long time too. Both are a big part of our success.

But I knew we still needed more help from a strategy and leadership perspective. We needed someone to prepare us to get ahead of the wave everybody saw coming. I didn't even know what you call that kind of person, but I knew they must be out there: someone to evaluate the business and then coach us on how to clean things up, restructure it and then manage the growth before it grew too complex.

Someone told me that what I was looking for was called a "business coach." What a great name! I imagined it would be like hiring a tennis coach to evaluate my game and then train me to understand strategy, hit the ball better and play the game better. Obviously, if a business coach is any good, they won't be around too long because they will have trained you how to think through your problems better and how to lead your team to success at the bottom line by driving the business towards the vision and by having more money in the bank account at the end of the month. That's not the kind of business coach Bob was, so it didn't work out as I had hoped, but looking back, it's clear that God put Bob in my life to gently humble my proud spirit. I wasn't cocky, but I was saying and doing things so people would praise and honor my self for being spiritually minded, and for being a good guy. My self loved that feeling, and I was often putting my own self above the self of others. In the business, that's called *pride*.

After a short time, Bob became our CEO and told me, "You know, Dave, you just need to work in your sweet spot, your strike zone, which is to focus on product design and that marketing stuff. You leave the hard business stuff up to the professionals." At the time, it sounded like music to my ears. So that's what I did.

But when I would ask question about things I didn't understand, Bob would slowly lean back in his chair, shake his head side to side and roll his eyes. Then he'd chuckle and say, "Dave, Dave, Dave . . . you hired me to help you, and I'm trying my best. But when you keep asking me these silly questions, that's called micromanaging." Then he would lean forward and say super slowly, "You need to learn something called *de-le-ga-tion*. You're paying me good money to do a job, and now you just need to trust me."

HOW TO GROW SALES THE EASY WAY

Even with Bob installed as CEO, I was still in charge of "silly marketing." My friend David Cheese had his master's in marketing and had been working in marketing for 20+ years, and he helped me understand some of the fundamentals of it all. First, he helped me rethink our website.

"Instead of trying really hard to get a whole lot of new visitors to your website," he told me, "why don't you try to convert more of the web traffic you already get?"

Of course, my first question was, "What does *convert* mean?"

He smiled. "To convert them from just being a looker into being an owner. How many people do you get to your website each day?"

We had about 1,000 people a day visit our website.

"Since you sell about 10 bags each day," he explained, "you probably have about a 1 percent conversion rate. That means about one out of every 100 people who visit your website buy a bag. What if, instead of trying really hard to get another 1,000 people to visit the website, you instead tried to go from one sale per 100 visitors to 2 sales per 100 visitors? That would be a 2 percent conversion rate, and your sales would double."

He went on, "Right now, you tell a lot of fun stories of your cool adventures around the world, and you have really nice pictures of your bags. You're hitting the emotional buyers really well. They say, 'Oh man, I really like this company. I want to buy something from them,' but you're missing out on the logical buyers. The guys who say, 'It looks good and the people seem honest enough, but am I going to be sorry I made this decision, or will I be happy? I need to understand it is true quality. Will it last? Is the value I'm going to get out of it worth the amount of money they're asking for it?'

"Something very important that helps logical buyers is if they feel you're a credible company. And they mainly gauge that by looking at how professional your website looks. So, first things first, Dave, you need to change your middle school extra credit project website and make it into a professional one. That will remove a lot of the doubt people have."

I thought David was probably right. So, right away, I got ahold of my friend Tim Haskins in Portland. His company, Copious Creative, had built a lot of websites for really big companies. Since he knew me and my story personally, I felt he could make us a great website that matched our brand and told the story well.

Right away, he told me I needed better photography. At that point, I was doing all of the photography on the tailgate of my truck. Right about then, my beloved nephew, Aiden Franklin, asked if I would hire him to do our product photography, even though he hardly knew anything about photography. Still, everything Aiden had ever tried turned to gold, so I knew I could count on him. He had been a pro skater and then started touring around the country as the lead singer of a successful band, but he felt it was time for a little more stability for his family. He quickly learned the ins and outs of photography, and his photos were amazing.

On September 14th, we launched our new, warm and professional website that shared our stories for our emotional customers, while at the same time taught our logical customers about leather and quality. That, combined with the new rich and professional photos, changed everything. The website launched and our sales went up 30 percent overnight and never changed. We quintupled sales for the year, from $250,000 in 2007 to $1,250,000 in 2008.

We quickly realized we needed more production and more consistent quality than we were getting from Hanz.

OPENING A LEATHER FACTORY

Since Bob had been a supervisor at a big industrial company for 10 years, he convinced me he was an expert in all things manufacturing. So, we decided to partner with him in creating a leather factory in Mexico. On October 13th, 2008, Bob and I opened True Blue Production.

Now that Bob and I were 50/50 partners in the factory, we agreed he would be responsible for all finances and production and I would be in charge of sales and marketing to bring new clients in once we got our own quality up to snuff. (By the way, if you google "50/50 partnership," you will find a ton of lawyer ads and lawyer websites saying, "Do 51/49, but *never* 50/50.")

Suzette and I knew a nice man living in Leon, let's call him Richard, and hired him to be our general manager. He found a building and then hired 14 people away from the Dooney and Bourke factory to start making our leather bags. Many of those original people are still with us today, like Luis, Adriana, Jaime, and Arnulfo.

Shortly after we opened True Blue Production, we stopped ordering bags from Hanz's factory, but that didn't slow down his production of our bags. A customer sent me a link to www.saddleback leather.us. Hanz had cloned our website, word for word, and started selling my exact bags. When I confronted him, he pretty much told me to go screw myself.

I paused and said, "Hanz, if you don't stop this right away, then I'm going to tell your dad about all of the illegal things you're doing, and that would make him ashamed to know he has a criminal for a son. Do you love money so much that you'll lower yourself to this level?" His clone website was down a few days later.

Hanz was the first unethical and creatively bankrupt person to knock us off, but he wasn't the last. It wasn't long before I found 19 different companies selling exact replicas of my first leather bag. Imitation is the ultimate form of flattery, and I was flattered at first. But again, the prophetic words of that business consultant came rushing back: "Diversify your product offering and establish your brand, or you'll go out of business."

CROSS X

On April 6th, 2009, Cross Xavier Munson was born and we loaded him up in that same shiny Toyota Tundra as we did Sela and drove him home from the hospital. At first, I thought, "Man, how could I love any other child more than I love Sela?" But in no time at all, I loved Cross just as much.

On April 27th, when Cross was all of 3 weeks old, we got him his first passport and embarked on his first international trip of many. We flew to Washington, DC, took a train to Maryland and then took a taxi to where our new to us, imported from Scotland, 1984 Land Rover Defender 110, complete with a spare tire on the hood, was waiting. It was so cool looking.

We loaded our luggage into the back and drove straight to Niagara Falls, where the Land Rover broke down. In the Land Rover world, they say breaking down is part of their charm. Thankfully, we found a Land Rover mechanic on the Canada side of the falls, named Paul Safari, who got it up and running in no time. From there, we drove through Canada to meet a couple who were customers, Eddie and Lerryn Dejong whom we had become friends with online. We then dropped down to Chicago to see my brother, Jonathan, graduate from Wheaton College and then drove back home to San Antonio, Texas.

That Defender was cool looking, for sure, but totally undependable and perpetually in need of one $2,000 repair after another. In Africa they say, "If you want to go far out into the bush, drive a Land Rover. If you want to get back, drive a Land Cruiser." They also say that if an English car isn't leaking oil, the reason is because it's out of oil. Do you know why the British stopped making televisions? Because they couldn't figure out how to make them leak oil. But that Defender sure did look cool.

It was red and white, but I had it painted a dark Land Rover green and it came out perfectly. I then threw the seats into the back of our Toyota Tundra and drove them to Mexico to be reupholstered with our same Saddleback Tobacco tan leather. Oh my gosh! That thing looked amazing, and people couldn't stop talking about it and taking pictures wherever I parked it.

As soon as Jonathan graduated from Wheaton, he jumped right back into the company to help. This time with PR. And did he ever help. I quickly learned that my brother is a networker, connector and salesman, and he did PR about as well as anyone could. He started a "Man Bags" group on The Art of Manliness forum, got me 2 interviews on Fox News and got people writing about us in magazines, on news websites and a thousand places in between. He did an amazing job, and our popularity and sales grew and grew from there.

With basically just a two brother marketing team, Saddleback again quadrupled sales, going from $1.25 million in 2008 to over $5 million in 2009, and that sales trajectory stayed steep and strong all the way to 2013. I don't know if I can stress this enough: If you sell stuff online, you *must* have a strong PR member on your marketing team.

LEARNING LOVE AND RESPECT

By September 2009, Suzette and I had been married for 3 years, and we'd been fighting for about half of those waking hours. Our routine was this: On Monday, we'd fight and then apologize to each other and then have no fighting on Tuesday. On Wednesday we would start fighting again and then apologize, and Thursday would be a day of peace, but Friday was coming. Since we had agreed that *divorce* was not even a word to whisper, we resolved to live out the rest of our lives being miserably married half the time and laughing our heads off and having a blast the other half.

One night after a fight, I was ignoring Suzette completely until about 12:30 a.m., when she came into the living room and softly asked if I were coming to bed. Without looking up from my laptop, I told her coldly, "No, I'm busy."

That's when she said, "Hey, Dave, this marriage isn't working. We need to go to marriage counseling."

I wholeheartedly agreed and figured that if we went, the counselor would recognize all of her jacked up thinking and fix her. Then our marriage would be all better. Of course, she was thinking the exact same thing about me.

Then she said, "But I was praying and I feel God wants us to read that marriage book we have upstairs, *Love and Respect.*"

"Okay", I said, "we'll start reading it tomorrow."

"No," she said, "I feel like we're supposed to start reading it tonight."

So, I went upstairs, grabbed it off the shelf and met her on our bed to read it together. We read the first 2 chapters out loud that first night and couldn't believe what we were reading. It was as if the author had been listening to our arguments and conversations and then wrote a book about our marriage. Really, he was writing about our pride, because the Bible says there's no conflict without pride.

That book completely changed our marriage. And then, when we started talking about the book, people came out of the woodwork telling us how it had completely changed their marriages too. Even couples who had gotten to the point of signed divorce papers said it had kept them together.

According to the book's author, Dr. Emerson Eggerichs, generally, husbands desire to be respected more than loved and wives desire to be loved more than respected. He explained a lot of the ways well intentioned men are unknowingly unloving to their wives and a lot of the ways well meaning women are unknowingly disrespectful to their husbands. According to Eggerichs, when a man is unloving to his wife, she subconsciously says to herself, *That sure was unloving. I'm going to try to train him and help him learn to be more loving.* And then she does something that, to him, is disrespectful, but to her is the right thing to do.

Then he turns around and says to himself, *Dang, what she just said or did sure was disrespectful. I'm going to ignore her or say something so I can train and teach her to be more respectful.* And therefore, she is disrespectful and so he is unloving and then she is disrespectful and on and on and on they go in the Crazy Cycle. Understanding that dynamic and what those unloving and disrespectful things were changed our marriage. And though we've had a lot of fights since then, we don't have them nearly as often.

Alive in Africa

Back in 2008, something happened that expanded our world in unexpected ways. I received a quarterly magazine from my alma mater and read an article about a ministry called Africa New Life Ministries. What caught my attention was that one of my classmates was now their executive director, and they were doing a lot of great things. I closed the magazine, handed it to Suzette and said, "Hey, honey, look through this and see if there's anything interesting to you."

She found the same article about how Africa New Life worked with vulnerable women and children in Rwanda who were survivors of the 1994 genocide, where almost 1 million people were murdered in 90 days, but the genocide actually kept on going until 1998. Africa New Life helped orphans and street kids with education through a child sponsorship program, but they also had a sewing program for single mothers.

About 10 minutes later, Suzette told me that the Africa New Life article had really spoken to her and that we needed to talk with someone right away. That was music to my ears and, in no time, Saddleback got involved.

Now fast forward to August 2010, when our lives changed forever. The executive director of Africa New Life invited us to visit Rwanda and see the ministry that we'd been donating to for the last two years. What a great idea! We'd take this epic trip to get cool product pics and videos in all kinds of cool places and see the ministry too. This was going to be a blast.

Our first stop was Barcelona, Spain, where I got a great little video of our Leather Notebook Cover on top of some downtown hotel. From there, we flew to The Seychelles, an island nation a little north of Madagascar, off the coast of Somalia. I got a great little video of our iPod Case in the clear, blue waves crashing over my back. From The Seychelles, we flew to Tanzania for safari and to see The Great Migration in the Serengeti. That was cool because I videoed Suzette explaining our new Small Toiletry Case while in the background thousands of wildebeests and zebras crossed the Mara River with crocodiles snapping at them.

THROWING SPEARS WITH THE MAASAI

While we were on safari, we came across a Maasai village where they lived in dung huts, had a lot of wives and where everybody carried a spear. Well, I'm not one to let a great opportunity go to waste, so I arranged a little product demonstration video that involved their spears. This is the story I wrote for our web page about the Squared Backpack ("The Tank"):

Next to the Zulus, the Maasai are the most renowned tribe in all of Africa. Ernest Hemingway and even H. Rider Haggard wrote about this fierce warrior tribe who were legendary with the spear. It's not an accident that they've survived for so long.

But as my mom used to tell me, "Talk is cheap, son. Put up or shut up." You'd think I was pretty tough, too, if I carried around a big, long

Dave teaching English at Centro NOE in Mexico 1999

Dave with his original leather bag celebrating Y2K in Mexico City

Jim, Jake and Dave after a hard day hitchhiking in 2000

Original leather briefcase in Taxco, Mexico 2001

Dave and his brother Jonathan in Tecomatepec, Mexico 2001

Blue's stud fee puppies traded for 100 tacos in 2001

Marketing trip to Bled, Slovenia in 2005

 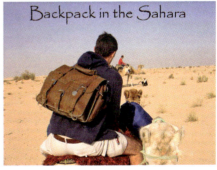

North African Colosseum 2005   *Tunisian camel journey 2005*

Prague, Czech Republic 2005

Blue in West Texas 2005

Leather Briefcase in Hungary 2005

Mexican Federale Bag 2005

Santa Elena Canyon, Big Bend National Park 2006

Suzette's MySpace pic gutting a deer 2006

Dave and Suzette preparing for the honeymoon

Bora Bora honeymoon marketing trip 2006

Dave and Suzette working on their honeymoon 2006

Sharkdiving 60 ft. below on the honeymoon

Hubba Hubba! Dave's hot wife with a knife strapped to her leg 2006

Crocodile testing in Australia 2006

Male kangaroo in Australia 2006

Daddy-Daughter date in the Seychelles 2010

Manchild Cross Munson in the Seychelles 2010

Suzette meeting Tanzanian Maasai tribe in 2010

Coming home from safari to our excited son 2010

Spear throwing contest winner of the Maasai 2010

Suzette with Mountain Gorillas in Rwanda 2010

Dave with the Silverback in Rwanda 2010

Dave and Sela heading out to the African bush 2010

Suzette getting addicted in Kageyo, Rwanda 2011

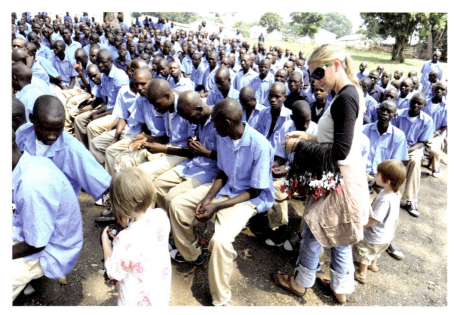

Munsons handing out cross necklaces on Iwawa Island, Rwanda 2011

Mama and babies in Real de Catorce, Mexico 2011

A Giraffe Manor breakfast in Kenya 2012

Waiting for the plane in the Maasai Mara, Kenya 2012

Munsons in front of their tent home with ChiChi and Mongo 2015

Dave's home office at their tents 2015

Munson family trying to blend in in the Sahara 2015

Father-Son Sahara chess match on the Leather Chess Set 2015

The naked and afraid Munson family in Hawaii 2016

Dave's office at the Saddleback Headquarters

Nervous lions with Dave and Suzette in Zambia 2022

Saddleback Leather, The Official Leather Goods of the Texas Rangers

Dave, Suzette, Sela and Cross with wild elephant in Zambia 2022

Dave and Suzette on Day of the Dead 2023

Munson sons and daughters-in-law in Rwanda 2023

Saddleback designed 1794 Limited Edition Toyota Tundra 2024

Cross Munson in CEO training in Zambia to take over one day 2024

Suzette and Sela on their 30th trip to Africa 2024

spear and talked about how I killed a lion with it to become a man and how even my smell and the sound of the little jingly things on my skirt scares the lions away. But it's another thing to show it. So, I took the family to the middle of nowhere Tanzania and demanded to see some action behind all the legendary tough talk. This is how it went down.

We drove in a cool Toyota Land Cruiser to a cold, high elevation Maasai village near the Ngorongoro Crater. The chief wasn't there, but the eldest of his 35 sons, Daniel, was and oh, how he loved my leather backpack and satchel. So much so, he insisted on carrying them. He spoke English and so went on and on about my pigskin lined leather backpack and satchel. He couldn't believe such a thing existed, made out of cow and pig.

He went on to explain and show us their daily lives and also explain how their multiple wife system worked. He only had 2 wives, but his dad had ten because he had enough cows to provide for them. And I thought just having Suzette was complicated enough. I asked Daniel about their spears and how they protected their people and animals with them. He showed me how they held their spears to most efficiently fight off the lions and leopards and hyenas. I asked whether they ever threw their spears. He told me they did, but only when they were in a group because if you're alone and you throw your spear at a lion and miss, you're dead meat.

That's when I announced the backpack spear throwing contest, and the winner got my Leatherman multi-tool. The one who could best run a spear through my backpack from a distance was the winner.

So, I hung my Squared Backpack on a tree and the men took turns throwing their spears at it. But they weren't just competing for the Leatherman. Daniel told me that part of the way a man attracts a wife is by proving he is the most capable in protecting and providing for their wives and children. How high they can jump, how far they can run and how many cows they have for milk are all factors. And how well they can throw their spear to pin a leather backpack to a tree was now another. From what I experienced, all of what Ernest Hemingway, H. Rider Haggard and so many others said about that fierce and highly skilled, spear wielding African tribe was well deserved. And I've got the spear holes in my backpack to prove it.

After a few weeks, we flew to Rwanda to go gorilla trekking, where I did a video description of the Front Pocket ID Wallet while standing right in front of a giant Silverback gorilla.

LOVE 41

In Rwanda, we finally got to see the Africa New Life ministry. And that's where the record came screeching to a halt. Our eyes were opened and tears started flowing. Of that long, 8 week trip, easily the most impactful and life changing part was our 3 weeks in Rwanda.

One of the things we did when we arrived in Rwanda was to help serve basic meals to the hundreds of orphans and street kids who were living in and around the landfill but came through the program at Africa New Life every Tuesday and Thursday. We were surrounded by these hundreds of young boys and girls, and they all wanted a hug. It was overwhelming and neither Suzette nor I could keep from crying.

And that was when all of it went from my head to my heart. I knew all of the facts about the suffering and sadness in my head, but when I experienced it and hugged it and interacted with all of the kids, all of a sudden Jesus' teachings in the Bible and His love for me made a whole lot more sense. And then I started to think about my own children and personalized it.

I thought, *What if Suzette and I had been murdered and were lying there dead in front of our home, and Sela and Cross were just little and were standing there next to us trying to wake us up, but couldn't. And what if they were hungry and scared and they didn't know what to do and started wandering the street looking for food. Would I want someone to send them a check for food and education, or would I want someone to come and smile and hug their necks and spend time with them and love them and care for them?*

Both, of course, and that thought made the difference.

We were permanently changed by what we witnessed and experienced and through the relationships with our new children that started. In fact, just this morning, I was on a video call with two of our orphan boys, whom we call sons and whom we sponsored on that first trip and informally adopted into the Munson family. I remember saying to myself on that trip, *How did I not know about this all my life? How was I so oblivious?*

The one certainty from this first visit was knowing that we would be back.

In October of 2010, just 3 months after we got home, we went back to Rwanda, this time helping lead a large group from Austin, Texas. Within 12 months of our first visit, we had been to Rwanda 4 times and have gone 2 or 3 times most years since then.

We were on a mission. God gave us a sphere of influence, and we wanted them to experience what we did. I estimate we have brought about 400 customers, employees, friends and family members to visit their sponsored kids. And adding up our time in Africa, we realized we've lived on that continent for about a year and a half of our lives, 3 to 6 weeks at a time.

After donating to Africa New Life for a few years, Suzette deeply desired to get more personally involved in the lives of individual single mothers in Rwanda and with our own sponsored kids, whom she became a mother to. She knew they needed more and she wanted to do more, so she and her sister, Tina, started scheming about what they could do.

In late 2011, we were riding down the road in Rwanda with a church group from Austin, and Suzette was talking about her concept for a company. She thought Saddleback could develop a line of leather designs for women, which the profits could help those like the mothers and children we met in Rwanda. But Suzette was struggling to come up with a name. "Maybe 'Love For Children' or 'Love 4 One Child' or 'Love 4 One'"?

Immediately, the pastor of the church said, "I wonder what Psalm 41 says?" So, he looked it up and read the first 3 verses aloud:

> Blessed is the one who cares for the poor;
> the LORD will deliver him in the day of trouble.
> The LORD will protect and preserve him;
> He will bless him in the land and refuse to give him over to the will of his foes.
> The LORD will sustain him on his bed of illness
> and restore him from his bed of sickness.
> Blessed is the one who considers the poor! (BSB)

Well, that settled it: *Love 41* it was. In November of 2011, Love 41 became Saddleback's heart that we wore on our sleeve. Saddleback's slogan is "They'll Fight Over It When You're Dead." Love 41's is "Where Receiving Is Giving." It was an easy decision that 100 percent of the profits would go directly to helping orphans, widows and street kids, though we've always been giving from Saddleback because we believe what the Bible says. It says that the whole Earth is God's and everything in it. So, we believe that includes our home, kids, dogs, shoes and money too.

Suzette is one of those stylish women who has a great sense of the way things should look. She can dress cool casual or high street classy. So much so that her friends often ask her to take them clothes shopping. Before we met, people would fly her around the country to decorate their homes. So, it seemed only natural that as Saddleback grew, Suzette would easily put together some cool looking women's designs for the company.

In 2009, she said she'd give designing a try. Of course, I then gave her all of my guidelines for Saddleback's design style: Only use thick, stiff leather and thick, non-contrasting thread with double stitching; edges needed to be sewn outwards; and absolutely no zippers, buttons, snaps or any other breakable parts were allowed.

Despite these rules, Suzette designed several homeruns. But we saw a lot of returns on some of them for being too bulky and heavy. So, we rethought the rules in 2011. What if in Love 41, Suzette could design what she wanted for herself? She and her sister, Tina, started designing lighter, softer bags for Love 41, and lo and behold, they were popular, and she even uses zippers!

JOE THE FILMMAKER

In February of 2012, we took 14 of our employees and some of their family to Rwanda so they could understand more of what their work at Saddleback was really doing. The trip cost around $4,500 per person and we agreed to cover $3,000 if they covered $1,500 so they'd have a little skin in the game.

We announced it to the whole company and everyone was excited. About a month before the trip, I called up one of our part time customer service reps, Joe Callander, to see how coming up with the $1,500 was going. He said he could only come up with $500. He was living in Hollywood, California, as a struggling filmmaker, working part time for us and part time as a Vespa mechanic but just couldn't make it happen for the trip.

So, I asked him, "Joe, if we pay for the rest, will you document the trip and film some product stuff for us?"

He agreed and we started brainstorming ideas and planning the trip. I already had that nice, semi-pro Sony videotape camera that I'd used in Jamaica, and Joe listed a few more pieces of equipment we needed to bring along.

I had no idea how great adding Joe to the group would be. We hugged for the first time at the Kigali, Rwanda, airport and got settled in. The next day, Joe got out his notepad and showed me the "Shot List" he'd come up with to make our filming more efficient. I didn't even know a "Shot List" was a thing. I was impressed.

Joe stepped us up to a whole new level with our first professional video, "Searching for a Drum." He followed me going all around Rwanda searching for a drum to carry in my nice, big leather duffle bag, which we affectionately call "The Beast." I had no idea how good of a filmmaker Joe was until I saw what he came up with. I knew his dream was to become a big time filmmaker one day, but he proved he already was one. In his editing, he even included comedic pauses, hoping to make people smile and laugh. How great is that?

YOU SHALL NOT GO

By early 2012, we had been going back and forth to Rwanda, but it was definitely time for variety. "Suzette," I said, "imagine all of the cool content we could get if we went around the world and filmed a documentary on the design process and inspiration of how our canvas and leather Mountainback Collection came into existence?"

She loved the idea and hit the internet to start planning cool places to stay along the way.

I called Joe and told him, "We're leaving in a few months on a trip around the world and we'll be gone for about 2 months. We really want to get all we can out of it for Saddleback. Would you be up for going with us to document the whole thing and get some cool videos and photos for the company?"

After 5 seconds of silence he said, "Sure, I'd be up for that."

Joe and I started brainstorming product demo video and documentary ideas again, and Suzette started planning the flights, transportation and the coolest places she could find to stay, like the entire third floor of one wing of a Scottish castle built around AD 1200 with 14 foot high ceilings. It was cheaper than the local hotel and we even had an extra 4 bedrooms to spare. Finding cool places to stay is definitely Suzette's superpower.

I had Joe fly to our home in San Antonio, Texas, to brainstorm more and finalize the plan. That first night, he handed me his list of what he needed for the trip with a budget of about $40,000: $20,000 for gear and $20,000 to bring along a sound guy and a director of photography. Joe would be directing.

I laughed out loud and said, "Joe, things are kind of tight right now, so it's going to be a stretch for us to even go. We can buy the camera gear, but we can't afford for anyone else to go but you. Do you still want to go?"

With a concerned look on his face, he agreed. Later, Joe told me that was one of the best things that had ever happened to him.

Next, I brought it up to Bob that we were going to take a two month family business marketing trip around the world, and we were bringing our part time customer service guy, Joe, along to get some cool photos and videos in neat places.

Bob smiled, slowly shook his head and said, "Sorry, Dave, you can't go. We don't have the money for a trip like that. Things are really tight, and we owe the tannery a lot of money."

I gave him a stern, serious look and said, "Are you kidding me? If we don't have enough money to go on this trip, then something is really wrong. We're selling more bags than ever before. In fact, we're having trouble even keeping our best sellers in stock, and you're saying we don't have enough money to go on a trip? Listen, Bob, I'm not asking for your permission to go. We're going. I just wanted to let you know about it so you wouldn't wonder why I wasn't answering the phone."

I told him we would pay for the trip out of our own pocket and reimburse ourselves in December, when the Christmas sales were raging. He went on and on about what a bad decision it was and how irresponsible and reckless I was being.

It was that meeting that made me start questioning everything. I started to realize Bob didn't have as much wisdom as I thought he did. It was more than clear that something was majorly wrong.

Sadly, one major lesson I've learned over the years is that when I say to myself, *Something is wrong*, or *It just doesn't make sense*, over and over and over again in the same month, then that means something is definitely wrong, but I just don't know what it is yet. Time to dig in. Trust your intuition. It's there for a reason.

AROUND THE WORLD IN 62 DAYS

In June of 2012, we embarked on the journey, landing in Scotland to film all that we had learned from the last trip to the waxed cotton factory, Halley Stevensons in Dundee. And, of course, we filmed the Highland Games too. I had heard that they were one of the two highest quality waxed canvas manufacturers on the planet, so I asked the owner, Martin Wigglesworth, if they were the best in the world. He replied, "I wouldn't say we're the best, but I don't know anyone who does it better." What a great answer!

I had always wanted to develop the highest quality leather and canvas bag collection in the world, since I had always loved waxed canvas. It had an aged, weathered look that was so appealing to me. So, I asked a million questions of Martin.

He explained all that goes into a quality fabric. When he was a child, his parents would go down to the shipyards to get bales of the great cotton from India and weave it in their home on the looms. He studied textiles in university and had worked in the fabric industry his entire life. He said a great cotton fabric starts with the type of long staple cotton that only grows in certain regions of the world. It makes thinner yarn so more can be wound together to make a single stronger and tighter thread. The more strands, the better.

He also explained all about how the air in the cotton mill needs to be purified so dust and other impurities don't get spun into the fabric. There was a lot more about how they dye and wax and inspect. In other words, we learned a lot and filmed it all.

From there, we flew to Kenya to understand more about how people sew canvas to make their products last a long time under extreme conditions. And what better way to do "research and development" than to stay in canvas tents on safari.

It just so happened to be Sela's fifth birthday out in the Maasai Mara, when she got the best birthday present ever. We were way out in the bush, parked in a very cool modified Land Cruiser, with no sides or windows, when a leopard casually walked directly to Sela through the tall grass and about 5 feet away from her, stopped and stared her in the eyes for about 5 seconds and then slowly turned and walked away.

No one could believe it. I said, "Hey, Sweetie, that was a birthday gift from God to you." Whether the leopard was just considering eating her or it was a wink from God, it was very cool.

When we got back to Nairobi, we went to interview the greatest tentmaker in the world, Rob Flowers, of the East African Canvas Company, to learn about his seams to keep the water out. He was a British Kenyan guy who, for the last 25 years, had been designing and building strong, durable canvas tents that keep things dry on the inside. When we got to his headquarters, our jaws were gaping open. His offices, workshops and "showroom" were all big wall tents with either hardwood or concrete floors with sliding glass doors and windows. These were not smoke peyote, run naked through the woods, hippy yurt tents, but the kind of tent you would imagine Ernest Hemingway sitting on the porch of, sipping tea and writing one of his books. I didn't know tents like these existed. I asked a thousand questions and learned that it all boiled down to having great seams that kept the water out. I knew for sure that these tents would have to happen in my life somehow, I just wasn't sure how yet.

Next, Suzette had arranged for us to stay at a place called Giraffe Manor, where we got an epic photo with the giraffes stretching their necks through the dining room windows to eat off our breakfast table. That photo made it onto the front page of Yahoo News and then onto every major website east and west of the Mississippi, and the sales on our website shot up when it hit too.

From there, we flew to visit our Rwandan kids, since it was only a 2 hour flight away. From Kigali, we flew through South Africa and then east on to Australia to learn about kangaroo leather from the experts there.

I was still trying to decide what would be the best leather lining in the world to use, so I considered kangaroo, because it is known as the strongest and most durable leather in the world at its thickness. In Australia, kangaroos are just like cows, harvested for their excellent meat. At the same time, they are a huge problem and responsible for a large number of traffic deaths and other mayhem.

We visited a kangaroo tannery in Sydney where the owner explained to me, in depth, all about kangaroo skin's physical properties and fiber structure that make it the toughest leather in the world, at its thickness. The Aussies use it to make high end motorcycle riding suits, high quality soccer shoes and even shifting boots in expensive cars. I decided against using kangaroo skin to line Mountainback bags, but it was so interesting to learn about.

From Sydney, we kept flying east to Auckland, New Zealand, for the final interview. As we were feeding all of our leather suitcases, duffle bags and backpacks through the X-ray machine, a customs agent came out of his office with a smile and asked, "Hey, are you Dave from Saddleback Leather?"

"Yes," I responded.

He said, "I saw all of this gorgeous leather coming through and thought, *It can't be anybody else. It has to be the Saddleback Leather guy.* I have one of your briefcases and get compliments on it all the time. I love your stuff, mate." That was cool.

We then interviewed a man who had been making sails for ships his entire adult life. His father had learned the trade just after World War II, and he apprenticed under him. He explained all about how they sew the fabric of sails so they last for decades under constant, intense stress in heavy and hard winds. So much of it is in their stitching patterns and how they reinforce high stress points.

He said a sewing machine is a perforation machine, and if you have a row of holes too close together, the fabric will tear like the top sheet on a pad of paper. He said sailmakers use a big wide open zig zag pattern so they don't get that straight row of stitches. That and the other tricks of the trade and wisdom I gained from that man have influenced the way I think about how to design other things to last a long time.

I asked a few different people what it was about Kiwis that made such a small island nation so excellent at so many things. They said it is all in the mindset of the culture they are raised with. Everyone knows that when you do something, you do it right, because your life may depend on it. That's why New Zealand dominates the world in all things boating and sailing, not to mention rugby. Did you know that the New Zealand National Rugby Team, the All Blacks, since 1903, has the highest winning percentage of all sports teams who play internationally (76 percent) and is regarded as the most successful sports team in human history? It's because of their strong work ethic and the mindset that one should act like your life may depend on it.

And that's where our slogan for our Mountainback Collection came from: "For when your life depends on it."

HOME SWEET HOME

After 62 days, we finally got back home to Texas. Laying in our own beds never felt so good. I noticed that something had shifted for me and our company. The trip had moved us to a whole new level. The incredible and almost unbelievable photos and videos we'd gotten had cemented our brand as a serious but fun competitor in the industry. No one had ever seen anything like what we presented to the world, and it shaped our style of marketing for the future.

The trip also taught me a lot about design but also a lot about tents. Fast forward to 2015, when we had Rob Flowers make 4 tents and set them up in Texas for us to live in, hardwood floors and AC included. Our friends often tell us that we live in a resort and that our tents are nicer than their homes. Eleven years later, we're still living in them. But more about our tent home later.

In October 2012, not long after we got home, I called up Joe and said, "Hey, Joe, we all really love your work, so I want you to move to Texas and come on as our full time filmmaker."

It was quiet on the other end for a bit, and then he said, "But what would I do?"

I laughed and said, "Make films."

He started packing his bags within 2 seconds of hanging up. Bob thought it was a horrible idea and a total and complete waste of money, but hiring Joe Callander to be our full time filmmaker was one of the best business decisions I'd ever made. And even apart from the business aspect of things, we went through a lot together and became good friends.

How to Be the Boss

By March of 2012, the factory was still a jacked up mess. We were still producing excessively high quality bags because of the tough materials we used, but about two out of every 10 bags would have a crooked buckle, a misaligned strap or some recurring odd defect. It seemed obvious to me Bob didn't know what he was doing overseeing the factory, so I suggested to him that we bring in a consultant to help us get healthy. That's what humble, normal people do.

But Bob became furious. His ears turned red, he furrowed his brows and squinted his eyes and shouted, "Give me a break! Don't you think I know what I'm doing?"

To which I responded, "Well, the factory is a disaster. Tons of quality issues keep recurring, new ones keep slipping by, our shipments are always late, the bags are getting so expensive to make and we don't have any money in the bank. What do you think I think?"

In early December of 2012, Bob was in Georgia visiting family for Christmas when his 6 year old Range Rover broke down again and was leaking oil and needed another new engine after they had already had it rebuilt the year before. I didn't want to wait any longer. So, I flew there, met him at a restaurant and fired him on the spot rather than wait until he got back to San Antonio.

BIG SALES, NO MONEY

In January of 2013, just after selling a record $13 million at Christmas, we hardly had any money in the bank. I was so angry and called Bob, who co-owned the factory and was still managing the production of our goods, to hear his explanation. He said Saddleback had just paid off the $800,000 we owed the tannery and that's why we were almost broke. *What in the world?* How could we have ever come to the point that we sold so much and had so little in the bank?

Being tethered to someone I just fired made 2013 a very long and hard year. It was a year of refining out impurities and growing in wisdom and understanding and was an experience that I wouldn't trade for anything. But it was painful and humiliating for me.

CAN YOU SEE IT?

Saddleback was a mess and I didn't know how to fix it or know how to lead my own company. But there was this one guy who I had met the year before in Rwanda who maybe I could call.

Africa New Life Ministries (also known as ANLM) had asked for money from a big foundation. And the foundation said they would gladly provide the funds, but on one condition: that ANLM first go through the executive coaching program of a man named Larry Briggs. Larry was in his 60s and had been coaching CEOs and executive teams of hospital systems and global companies for 25 years. ANLM agreed and brought Larry in to train at their Portland headquarters before flying him to Rwanda to coach the leadership team there. We just happened to be staying at the ANLM guest house in Rwanda at the same time, and so we hung out for the week and became friends.

I wasn't sure if I had enough money to pay the guy, or if he would even entertain the idea of working with such a small business, but I asked anyway and he said yes. Larry was over the top encouraging, genuinely humble and filled with wisdom. Over the next year and a half, he and I met together, either in Portland, San Antonio or on the phone, at least 4 days a week. He didn't just tell me how to do things but showed me how and helped me to grow in my understanding of business and leadership. As you'll see, his company, Vision 2 Action (V2A), was aptly named.

Five of us attended a 3 day offsite meeting Larry put on. He began by sticking five big 2' x 3' pieces of paper on the walls around the conference room with 5 different words on the top of each: *People*, *Promotions*, *Processes*, *Products* and *Profits*. Then he said, "I want all of you to close your eyes and *imagine* you're getting into a time machine and you get out in 10 years. Give me the *visual* of what you *see* Saddleback Leather is like if everything went the way you would like it to go.

"Look over the accountant's shoulder and *see* what's in the bank. What are sales like? Oh, *look*! There you are sitting at your desk. What kinds of things are you working on? What has the marketing department accomplished and what are they known for? When you're walking through the customer service area, what do you *see*? What do you hear people saying while they're on the phone with customers and what are they known for? How many people are there? What are they doing? Tell me what you see in the warehouse and fulfillment area. What is your reputation online and with customers? How do they feel? What does Saddleback's product offering look like? How is the business structured? What does the IT area look like? What would you love to *see* in all the different areas of the business if everything goes right?"

That got our imaginations going.

The next day, Larry stepped it down to a more realistic time in the future. "Now I want you to imagine you step into a time machine and go 3 years into the future. When you get out, nobody can *see* you, but you can *see* what everybody is doing in each of the departments. You can even *see* yourself and what you're working on. What's going on? What do you *see*?"

Those time travel exercises were really effective. Together, we came up with a solid vision for the company. This future vision we developed has been a gigantic part of Saddleback becoming what it is today.

Larry said this phrase about a hundred times for the next year and a half: *"A powerful vision, regularly spoken, will pull for its own fulfillment."*

Never has a truer word been spoken. I didn't realize it way back in 2006, but when I typed out the two pages of what I saw would happen with Saddleback if Suzette quit her job and we moved to Mexico, that was a simple vision she jumped right in to get behind it because she could see it.

If you have a business, a church, a non-profit, a school or any organization, please please please write out a simple vision of what you would like to be known for in 10 years. Then go to 3 years. If you make it too complicated, it may never happen. But just give it your best guess. You can start with a simple 3 sentences of what you hope it will look like. Three sentences is better than zero sentences.

We spent a lot of time over those next few days writing down our little guesses and dreams on little sticky notes and stuck them to the big papers on the walls. Larry guided us as we discovered where we wanted to be and what we wanted to be doing. I still didn't fully understand how important it was to do what we were doing, but in 2023, I read through that same ten year vision and almost laughed out loud because of how close we were to hitting it. There were no revenue targets, but how the business would be functioning and what we would be focusing on and known for was accurate. The heavy machinery Case Caterpillar company's statement is all about their people and their values, but has no growth or money targets.

KNOW YOUR PEOPLE

One of the next things Larry taught me was that to be a great leader, I needed to understand what every role required. I didn't need to know *how* to do everything but just know what kind of work was being done and what was required in the different roles: Will there be a lot of time working with data? Creative problem solving? Being alone a lot? Interacting with strangers? Analyzing numbers? etc.

Next, Larry said I needed to know how each person was wired. What kind of work did they naturally gravitate to first thing in the morning? What kind of work gives them energy, and what kind of work drains them of energy? What kind of work makes them check the clock every ten minutes, and what kind makes them lose track of time? He said if they're spending most of their time doing the kind of work they're wired for, then they'll have energy at the end of the day and won't really feel like they're working all that much.

To know our people better, Larry suggested we use the Core Values Index personality test (CVI), which would help us understand what kind of work gives a person energy and what drains our energy. A friend of mine, Steve Hackett, who ran a $12 billion company, said they use that test all the time. No test is perfect, but any test is better than no test at all. The more you learn about you and your people, the easier it will be for everybody. Use any of them. Strengthsfinder 2.0, Myers-Briggs, Enneagram, DISC, you name it, it's good for you and your team to take. Most of these have some free version.

If your team's wiring doesn't match up to the work they're doing, it'll feel like you're herding chickens, and I know what that's like from experience. Believe me, it's no fun.

ASK GREAT QUESTIONS

Larry would often say, "Dave, great leaders ask great questions." So, for the next year and a half, he showed me just how to do that.

On our calls, I would say, "Hey, Larry, this situation is not good. What should I do?"

He would respond, "I don't know, Dave. That's a toughie. What do you think we should do?"

I would then go on to tell him what I thought we should do.

Then he would say, "That's a great idea, Dave. I like the way you think. What's the first thing we should do to start?"

He helped me understand that when someone comes up with a solution themselves, they pull way harder for it to succeed than if I had just told them what to do. Nowadays, if you were to follow me around the office, you'd hear me say, "Man, that's a tough one. What do you think we should do?" What I've found is, my team often has a better solution than I do.

Why don't more people lead by asking questions? I've found that most people aren't very interested in the self of other people. Most everyone I know would immediately jump into a lake to help someone out or support a friend in a desperate time, but it's rare to find someone who is on the lookout for someone to help or serve or who is even interested in knowing about the self of the people around them more deeply. What I've found is that most people just want to talk about their self or about how much they know so they can impress us with their self. I know because I am self-ish like that more often than I'd like to admit. Another way of saying someone is self-centered is to say they are prideful. They're synonyms. Those focused on the self of others as more important than their own self are called humble people. Pride is a problem we all have, but it takes different forms. It's not just bragging or being cocky. Pride is way more. Humility is way more. Search "Signs of Pride List" and you'll see what I've been writing about. Your pride is likely the root of all of your troubles in marriage, business and your family, like it is mine.

I found the art of asking questions helped me more than just about anything in my business life. A good friend of mine was about to file for divorce, and so Suzette and I asked Bill and Sally if we could spend some time with them.

Bill was the strong, silent type who was not good at conversation. In fact, the only times Bill would really talk much was when someone asked him a question about something he was interested in. Otherwise, he would just sit quietly. As you can imagine, that does not go over well in a marriage. After a week or so, Sally wrote Bill a stinging goodbye letter and drove away. In the letter, she said she felt like Bill was not interested in her, that he'd only married her so he could have a free maid and cook and you know what. She didn't think that he liked her or was even interested in her as a person.

A couple of days after Bill showed me the letter, I said to him, "You know, I know how Sally feels. I don't think you really like me either."

He looked confused. "Why do you say that?"

I responded, "Well, after all these years of knowing each other and spending countless hours together, do you know how many brothers and sisters I have?" "No," he responded. "Do you know if my mom and dad are alive or dead? Married or divorced? Do you know what part of work is hard for me and which is easy?"

He admitted he did not know any of those things about me. I said, "Do you know why you don't know those things? Because you're not interested in me enough to ask. You're not intertested in anybody else but your own self. You're one of the most self-centered men I know."

At first, he just stared at me. Then he admitted he didn't know how to connect with people, that it was hard and painful for him. My response? "Well then, let's practice some chitchat."

Right away, Bill said, "Chitchat is a worthless thing to practice and a total waste of time. I don't want to do it." I quickly responded, "Trust me on this one, Bill. My marriage is good and yours isn't. Let's practice asking each other questions."

For the next two weeks, on the commute to work, we practiced chitchatting. The rule was to ask 5 connected questions to the other person and they had to respond with short answers. The exercise was about asking questions, not about answering them, so I started with the most meaningless subject I could think of and asked, "So, do you like your shoelaces?"

"Yes," he responded.

"Do you prefer round ones or flat ones?"

"Round."

"Have you ever bought your own shoelaces?" I asked.

"I bought these," he responded.

"Why did you buy those? By the way, Bill, that's 4 questions."

"Because the shoes came with green ones and I liked red ones."

"Why red shoelaces?"

"Because I feel like red fits my funny personality and green are more serious."

"Oh my gosh, Bill!" I exclaimed. "That is so interesting that you care about your own style and personal brand all the way down to your shoelaces. Wow! I just learned something cool about you that explains a lot to me. I bet Sally has a lot of really cool things about her that you could learn, if you were ever interested in her enough to dig by asking questions."

He slapped his palm to his forehead, closed his eyes and leaned forward for about 15 seconds. He opened his eyes and said, "So, how do you like your sunroof?" What we discovered was that even on trivial topics like these, aspects of our stories and personalities emerged, providing us a window into another's life and a valuable way to connect.

Every morning, we practiced asking questions, and Bill improved. We laughed and laughed and our friendship deepened. About a month later, Bill went to Sally's parents' home, where she had been staying, and talked her into coming back. They started reading the greatest marriage book of all time, *Love and Respect*, out loud to each other, and Sally told us it was the most she'd ever heard her husband's voice, and it was wonderful.

Later that year, they went to her family's home for Christmas and she told me that Bill had become a new man. Instead of sitting silently on the couch waiting for people to ask him questions about his self, he became the life of the party. He was asking people questions left and right and had great conversations. And he laughed a lot. Like Larry predicted, learning to ask questions is a powerful tool.

ASK "BY WHEN"

Another great leadership technique Larry pounded into my head was to *always* ask, "By when?" He said my business would grow at the speed at which we make "by when" agreements.

This is how it goes. Every so often during a meeting, I'll ask, "In this meeting so far, what have we agreed to?" And then I keep my mouth shut.

Once someone states the agreement, I say, "Great, who's handling that one?"

When someone takes it, I say, "Oh, that's great. *By when* can we expect it to be done?"

If they tell me, "I'm not sure. It's kind of complex. It all depends on what our supplier can do," then I ask, "Yeah, that makes sense. *By when* will you be able to talk to the supplier to get their date so you can give us a date?"

They say, "I'll call them and dig into it and give you a date on Friday."

And I respond, "Great, I look forward to hearing the date on Friday."

At first, working with Larry was like drinking from a firehose, but over the next 18 months, he patiently walked with me, shoulder to shoulder, and showed me how to run the company by asking me the questions that I needed to be asking my people. He modeled it because he knew the best lessons are caught, not taught.

Before I knew it, I was sounding like Larry. The 4 key lessons I caught from him are:

1. Share my vision.
2. Know my people.
3. Ask questions.
4. Make agreements.

Larry knew if I could learn these most foundational leadership methods, the business would stand strong. I still don't do it all right, but his coaching made all the difference in shaping Saddleback into what it is today.

Independence Day

In January of 2014, we had just had record sales for Christmas and morale was high until we saw our bank balance. We had a small yet efficient team, but as per usual, we didn't hardly have any money in the bank and it looked like we were going out of business. I was so discouraged, and I didn't know if I wanted to keep on doing this business thing. Would we ever get a break or was this just the way business was and it would always be hard? I was deflated and needed some encouragement, and God knew it. That's when something incredible happened. The first Saddleback Leather short film, "Tim and Susan Have Matching Handguns," which was about our customer service manager and her husband, got into the Sundance Film Festival. Our filmmaker, Joe Callander, was a gifted storyteller whose hard work had finally paid off. Out of over 8,000 submissions to Sundance, his short documentary was one of the only 62 "Official Selections" that year to make it. The reason I asked Joe to make films is because I wanted people to *see* what we cared about rather than just hear us talk about what we cared about. It seemed more authentic. My friend Tom ran a big hotel for one of the most luxurious hotel chains in the world and he told me about a time when they did a big "Save the Rainforest" marketing push. The angle was, every night you stayed in their fancy hotel, someone somewhere planted a tree in the rainforest and you were saving the planet. He said they got huge backlash for it because everyone knew they didn't care about the rainforest, but it was just a fake "cause" marketing ploy to make money. We were not cause marketing but just showing everyone, through film, that we valued our people. We weren't Saddleback Leather Corporation, but rather, we were a company full of individual people who loved people. I feel making art is always a way better way of sharing those kinds of things.

I gave Joe the freedom to figure it out. And figure it out he did. At the same time, we used film to educate people on quality so they would see that we valued quality.

By this time, we had posted 222 videos on our YouTube channel, educating and entertaining the public, but we hadn't really had wild success with any of them. For years, though, I had had 2 ideas I wanted to educate people about. I wanted to teach our customers all about the small details that take our bags from medium quality to high quality and I also wanted to educate them on all of the little tricks of the trade that low quality bag makers use that make bags fall apart so quickly.

Joe and I sat on the back porch and smoked I don't know many cigars, endlessly brainstorming how to get each of these 2 concepts across. At first, I thought each idea was going to be its own video, but then the perfect idea finally came to mind. We would explain to those knocking off our bags all of the fine details that make our bags last so long and look better every year, and then tell them that they didn't need to do those things because they could use these tricks instead. We insulted them like, "This is even easier than beating your wife and kids!" or, talking about hardware: "You can nickel plate anything. You can even nickel plate your crack pipe."

We published the "How to Knock Off a Bag" video to our YouTube channel two days before we left for the Sundance Film Festival.

While we were there, the video rocketed into lower orbit. We knew it was funny and educational, but we only expected it would maybe get 12,000 views because it was 12 minutes long. It shocked us to see it getting more than 50,000 views *per day* and even got on the front page of YouTube under "Trending." And it kept going.

The next thing I knew, Kai Ryssdal from NPR *Marketplace* was interviewing me, and a ton of other publicity started pouring in. Even Seth Godin, the great marketing thought leader, whose blog I regularly read, emailed to congratulate me.

Here's what I learned: In order to produce a successful video like "How to Knock Off a Bag," which was our 223rd video, we had to release 222 pretty good videos first. You can't expect to have wild success until you've put your time in. The way you get good at playing guitar is by playing guitar. At public speaking by public speaking. The way you get good at creating videos is by creating a lot of videos. All these years later, I still hear from people that it was *that* video that helped them pull the trigger and buy a Saddleback bag.

When people ask me, "Dave, I want to grow my business and have dedicated and loyal clients like you have. What can I do to move in that direction?" I tell them to become an expert in their industry by learning all they can and then educate, educate, educate their customers about what to watch for and what to watch out for when making a decision. Inform them of the tricks low quality schlicksters use and then explain what goes into high quality products or services. Whether it is lawn maintenance, roofing, electrical work, engineering or orthodontics, people will see you as an expert and appreciate your help.

The film festival gave me hope that brighter times were on the horizon, but that only lasted until I got home and saw what a huge financial mess we were in again. We had just sold about $14,000,000 dollars worth of leather goods in 2013, but instead of having $3,000,000 dollars of profit in the bank, we only had about $300,000.

And that was after our huge Christmas sales. And every week that amount was getting lower.

That's when I decided there had to be a full and complete reset. We had to be the sole owners of our own leather factory so we could control 100% of the supply chain and the business from start to finish. So, we hit the reset button and bought out Bob's half of True Blue Production. That 4th of July was like no other for us. We felt more independence and freedom than we had felt in years. We were now the proud owners of our own leather factory, and we renamed it Old Mexico Manufacturing. It felt so good.

The problem was that we still owed a lot of money to our hardware and leather vendors, and we were about two weeks away from not being able to pay our employees. We were sailing in rough seas, which I am weirdly honestly thankful for. Who gets the chance to learn this kind of stuff? What book could I have read or class could I have taken to deeply internalize and learn the lessons I learned here? And this is when those wise words from the VW repair shop owner came back to me. "You know Dave, I bet there are a lot of people who would trade their problem for your problem in the snap of a finger". He was right. I had a loving wife and healthy kids. We would be okay.

The way I think about hard times is with just straight-up logic. I believe that the Bible is 100% true, based on historical evidence, hundreds of fulfilled prophecies, numerous other facts and faith. Therefore, if God says it in the Bible, I believe it. I always think it's odd when people believe the founder of some religion who tells them that God told them something and that they just have to trust them and not question anything. It's good to understand why we believe something. But based on the facts, I believe 100% of whatever God says is true. Including this little nugget. "Rejoice at all times. Pray without ceasing. *Give thanks in every circumstance*, for *this is God's will for you* in Christ Jesus" (1 Thessalonians 5:16-18). So I was thankful.

He also said, "And we know that *God works all things together for the good* of those who love Him, who are called according to His purpose" (Romans 8:28). I was comforted knowing that whatever happened next, we were going to be better off. As they say, rough seas make good sailors.

But I had more reason to be fine in all this. God also wrote to me in the Bible, "*Consider it pure joy*, my brothers, when you encounter trials of many kinds, because you know that the testing of your faith develops perseverance. Allow perseverance to finish its work, so that you may be mature and complete, not lacking anything. Now if any of you lacks wisdom, he should ask God, who gives generously to all without finding fault, and it will be given to him" (James 1:2-4).

In Romans 5:3-4, He says, "Not only that, but we also rejoice in our sufferings, because we know that suffering produces perseverance; perseverance, character; and character, hope." God was shaping me to have a humble heart like Jesus's heart. I thought it would be a faster process after all of these years, but He's still working on my pride and this time was part of it.

Upon becoming the full owner of the factory, I fired almost all of the management and brought in a fresh new team. We set up payment plans with the tanneries, and I took over the books. A ray of light started peaking through the dark clouds, and our future slowly started looking brighter. We were almost immediately profitable again like we were back in 2009.

Tents and Terrorists

In January of 2015, I announced that we decided to move Saddleback Leather from San Antonio to Fort Worth, Texas. We wanted to centralize operations and have a headquarters to host visitors, get healthier and enjoy each other more by working face to face.

Fort Worth made the best sense for many reasons. My sister was shipping and receiving our bags from there, my parents and another sister lived in the area and the city was known for its traditional family values. Of all the major cities in Texas, Fort Worth gets the most snow, receives the most rain (after Houston), gets the least sticky air, is safest for crime, has the lowest cost of living, is the least crowded and is a direct flight to almost anywhere in the world. Why would we choose anywhere else?

Until now, working from home was all we'd ever known. Our employees were scattered across 12 states. I had bragged about the benefits of a distributed workforce in interviews to various media outlets for years, but it was time to mature as a business.

We were becoming bureaucratic. Simple things took a ton of time and energy to decide or to get done. What would normally be figured out in a few minutes by leaning in the doorway of someone's office often took several days because we had to schedule conference calls and meetings, sometimes a week in advance.

What Cicero said about life also applies to business: "The great affairs of life are not performed by physical strength or activity or nimbleness of body, but by deliberation, character, expression of opinion." And we would do a lot more deliberating and sharing of opinion when we were physically in the same space.

Camaraderie, decision making and creative ideas often happen when eating lunch together or hanging out after work. We also couldn't see each other's faces to naturally ask what, "What's wrong?" or "How was your daughter's ballet recital on Saturday?" Caring about the self of others is not just limited to poor and vulnerable people around the world.

We were so committed to moving everything to Fort Worth, I told everyone, that my family had just bought some land outside of town to build a house on. And my dream was to build the coolest headquarters in the whole world, not the biggest, not the most efficient, not the most expensive but definitely the coolest. I had lots of ideas: above ground tunnels, swinging bridges, catwalks, spiral staircases, hidden rooms and secret passageways. Lots of fire had to be in there too. And I wanted it to look and feel so incredible that people would pay top dollar just to have their wedding in our warehouse or showroom. The coolest idea is to build it out of big, fat, solid bales of leather scrap. Imagine that, of the billions of buildings that have ever been constructed on Earth, ours will be the first one ever made out of leather. Why not? And it's happening now.

THE COOLEST HOUSE IN TEXAS

In February of 2015, on the way back from one of our company trips to Rwanda, our family stopped off in Morocco for a fun little marketing trip. Morocco is literally synonymous with leatherwork. In Spanish, the name *Morocco* is "Marruecos" and *leatherwork* in Spanish is "marroquineria" because Morocco was known through the centuries as the global home of leatherwork, and they did not disappoint.

We flew into Marrakesh and stayed for a few days in a *riad* (a home with a courtyard) in the 2,000 year old walled "Old City" so we could walk the vast markets. I'd never seen so much leather in one place in my life. It was almost unbelievable. We then drove over the Atlas Mountains to the Erg Chebbi dunes to stay with the Tuaregs in the Sahara Desert (Sahara means desert in Arabic, so send that one to the Department of Redundancy Department).

Suzette arranged to have 4 camels waiting to carry us through the vast Sahara to our awaiting Bedouin tents. I don't use the word *awesome* very often, but when we rank and compare all the "business trips" our family has taken, Morocco ranks among one of the 2 most awesome. Even though it was so very cold at night and the heavy blankets weighed us down, the tents were cooler than cool, and the wall to wall rug floors and walls made it feel really cozy. It made me think, *I could get used to tent life*," and eventually, we did.

On March 15th, 2015, we moved from San Antonio to live with my mom and dad in their house just north of Fort Worth, and I began working with an architect to design our new home. Ever since I'd taken a drafting class my junior year in high school, I had dreamt of one day designing my own home and now was the time.

Before I started working with the architect, I prayed, "God, would You help us to have the coolest house in Texas?" I didn't want the most expensive or the biggest, but I wanted the coolest. The Bible says, "You have not, because you ask not," and so I asked. And the coolest house is what we got, but not in the way we were planning.

By May, Suzette and I had agreed on the style of the house being a plain, rectangular, two story, symmetrical Old English Country Home that looked like a shoebox with a roof. It was going to be plain and simple on the outside, but cool on the inside. Of course, I wanted hidden passageways, tunnels and secret rooms behind moving bookshelves, stuff like that. By the way, it doesn't take much more effort or money to be among the best in a category or design super cool, you just have to plan for it. So, I started working with the architect on the plans, and I was having so much fun.

We knew the house was going to take awhile to build, and it was a little crowded at Mom and Dad's house. But instead of renting a house for a year until our new house was ready, I said to myself, *Why don't we get one of those big safari tents, like Rob Flowers has as his office in Kenya?* We could resell the tent after we were done with it or it could be our Saddleback remote office. I ran the idea by Suzette, and she was fully onboard. She's that kind of a woman.

Rob said the 2 story tent that I designed would take too long for him to engineer. So, we decided on a couple of large individual tents instead. As Suzette and I talked through our needs, she said, "Well, it sure would be nice if we had one more tent for laundry and cooking so we wouldn't have too much noise or smoke from the stove in our bedroom. And what are we going to do when guests come to visit? For sure we'll need a smaller tent for them."

So, 2 more tents.

After finalizing the right dimensions and placement of the tents, our friend Russell Roberts managed to build the deck system for the tents to sit on. In July, Rob and his friend Andrew flew over from Kenya to set the tents up. And they turned out way cooler than we had ever imagined.

We ended up with 4 beautiful wall type tents with about 2,000 total square feet of living space. They sat on decks, 2 or 3 feet off the ground, and were built in a crescent shape, centered on a pond. Everyone who came by asked if they could take pictures. And I mean *every single person.* These tents are what you would imagine Ernest Hemingway or Theodore Roosevelt using while on safari, sitting on the deck, smoking an old pipe and writing in a journal.

It wasn't rough living in the tents. In fact, a lot of our friends who have stayed with us tell us that our tent home is nicer than their house or that it felt like they were at a resort. We have indoor toilets, hardwood floors, heat and AC and every night, come rain, snow, ice or heavy wind, we get to shower outside under the stars. I've actually slipped on the ice in the shower a few times and who knows how many venomous Copperhead snakes we've killed in the shower. Heck, I've killed 2 of them with a shampoo bottle.

Somehow, the Dallas / Fort Worth CBS news station heard about what we were doing and sent a camera crew to do a story on us. They called their weekly segment "Texans with Character."

On August 12th, 2015, we moved into the tents and didn't stop smiling for about a month. One of our favorite things is when there's a steady and gentle rain at night, the sound is so relaxing. Sela was 8 and Cross was 6 when we moved in, and they loved it too. We got rid of our TV and the internet was terrible, so we had more time for playing games and reading books together at night.

Since each tent is 50 feet from the next one, we have to walk down the deck to get snacks or move the laundry. It's almost impossible to not look up or around to admire nature, day and night. Orion's Belt and Mars are super obvious almost every night, and sometimes one of the kids will tell us to come outside to see the neat cloud pattern in the moonlight.

We enjoyed living in the tents so much that when we started talking about moving into the traditional home I had just designed, we all got kind of sad. We realized we were already living in the coolest home in Texas, for us. I canceled the final architectural drawings of our dream home and we've been in the tents 11 years now.

Later in 2016, our tents made it onto national television. My nephew, Aiden, shot a video of each room of the tents, and Joe took some of the other footage we'd shot on our phones and edited it all together. We loved it and put it right up on YouTube. Two days later,

I was contacted by a national midday show that thought their audience would think it was pretty cool and asked if they could air the video. And that popularized the tents and got us into *Texas Monthly*. We were also featured on a bunch of websites and did a ton of interviews and podcasts because of them. The great marketing benefit that came about because of the tents more than paid for what they cost us.

BACK TO THE ORIGINAL VISION

It was 2015, and with Bob out of the way, we could finally develop the factory with the original vision Suzette and I had in mind when we first envisioned building the factory back in 2008. We had always wanted to show great love to our people, in life changing, tangible ways, but Bob, who always agreed that we should do it, always also told us we couldn't afford to. But now, with nobody to stand in our way, we were marching forward toward the vision.

A few years earlier, we were in Rwanda and found out that some of the 70 women in the sewing center were so desperate to learn a trade that they felt they had no choice but to lock their children in their mud huts while they learned how to sew at ANLM's Women's Empowerment Center. It was common for women to walk 3 to 4 hours each way to get the free training, but hoping their child was still okay when they got home.

When Suzette heard this was happening, she jumped into action and told her sister, Tina, who had run a daycare for many years, that they needed to mobilize our Saddleback and Love 41 community to donate toys and equipment or commit to donating $10 per month so these women could have a healthy and clean place to leave their children while they trained. Thanks to the generosity of our customers, the daycare wasn't just a good one, it was the best one in Rwanda. The kids were growing intellectually, eating well, learning English and being loved. The support of our Saddleback customers was overwhelming. We've found, over the years, that when they see a need, they act.

It could have been the Dave and Suzette Show, and we could have funded some of it, but then it would have become dependent on us and also our Saddleback community would have missed out on the blessings that come with getting involved. God has given us a voice to speak to an army of generous people who buy our leather goods and who want to help and get involved, but sometimes they just need to know a trustworthy place to do that.

In September of 2015, Suzette saw the need for a daycare at our own factory too. So, she spearheaded it again and opened Leoncitos Daycare just down the street from our leather factory in Mexico.

Four months after it opened, I was in the conference room at the factory when our HR manager walked in with one of our stitchers from the production floor. His name was Genaro, and he spoke slowly with a quivering voice, with tears, "My wife and I moved to Leon to find work and every Sunday night, we left our 3 little children far away at my mother-in-law's house and they would cry and beg us not to leave them again. Then on Friday, after work, we rushed over to pick them up again. We did that because we were desperate and didn't have a place for them to be while we both came here to work. But now they are both at the free daycare you opened. Why did you open the daycare for free? Please tell me why."

There wasn't a dry eye in the room.

I put my hand on his shoulder and explained how God loved him and how God uses people to show His love for us. God had put it in our hearts to open this daycare, and the way we show our love to Him is by obeying what He puts on our hearts to do. "God shows you His love so you will want to get to know Him better. He gives us gifts, not because we deserve them, but because He loves to give gifts. That's called *grace*." It was a beautiful moment.

Next, we opened up a 4 year English school, Centro NOE Leon, for our factory workers, their kids and the kids in the neighborhood. *NOELEON* is a palindrome, so it was meant to be. Remember, when I first moved to Mexico, I taught English at Centro NOE in Morelia, which was when I had my first bag made? Back then, I saw how much of an impact learning English had on the lives of thousands of kids and their families. So, I thought it would be great to have a Centro NOE in Leon too. I reached out to the executive director at NOE International, Brian Overcast, and set it all in motion. Turns out, one of my students from 15 years earlier, Seydel, became our first NOE director in Leon.

Meanwhile, we still had not made a decision about the new headquarters. In October of 2016, my sister Patricia and I were looking to buy a building that could house the "coolest" headquarters, but somehow we ended up leasing a white rectangular, very industrial concrete shoebox with no windows except at the doors. If I ever become president of the United States, I'm going to pass a law requiring warehouses to have a lot of windows and be forced to pass a beauty threshold before they receive a certificate of occupancy. Not only was the stupid warehouse expensive, but it was way bigger than we needed.

Leasing that space for 6 years is one of my big regrets in life. Of course, I guess if that's as big as my regrets get, that's pretty good. Living out that 6 year long prison sentence served as a catapult to what's going on with the new headquarters we're building now in 2025.

VACATIONING WITH TERRORISTS

In March of 2017, on the way back from a trip to Rwanda, we stopped by a little island off the northeast coast of Kenya called Kiwayu, which was an island of Kenya, but directly across, on the mainland, was the disputed area of Somalia, that the British took away from Somalia and gave to Kenya several years before. The Somalis still claimed it as their own and their al-Shabaab terrorists were making it terribly hard on Kenya to occupy it. But technically, on maps, it was Kenya. I didn't know all of that. And something else I didn't know was that the US Department of State warns people to *never* go there. I saw that warning on the State Department's website when I got back to internet service.

I wrote the following in a product description for our customers on the website:

We finally get to our destination, called Mike's Camp, run and owned by a British Kenyan guy named Mike, a charming chap who had made a barefoot luxury Gilligan's Island style resort built almost entirely from woven reeds. The walls and floors were 100 percent woven and the ceilings were thatched, all of it supported by just branches and sticks.

It was super cool. I guess that's why billionaires stay there. Apparently, they fly in at low tide, land on the beach and walk up the sand dunes to the camp. Since we're not billionaires, we flew into Lamu and then took the little skiff for 2 hours to the island. Mike's Camp is where you completely unplug. So, I left the briefcase in Rwanda but brought a leather backpack, and as my man bag, the Indiana Satchel.

On our last full day there, we met a couple from Scotland at breakfast who had sailed to the camp on a dhow (sailboat) with their dreadlocked Kenyan/Somalian captain. I went over to introduce myself, since he seemed like a nice enough fellow, but I knew there was something wrong since he already had a beer in his hand at 8 a.m. and his eyes were empty.

Just after noon, coming back from a seashell hunting trip gone bad (that the family still whines about today), we met the dreadlocked captain at the dock. I walked straight up to him and told him this: "I just feel like God wants me to tell you something."

He drew close and replied, "Go ahead and tell me, man."

So, I did. I told him, "Omar, I feel like God wants me to tell you that he's really in love with you and that he thinks about you all the time and that he really wants to have a personal relationship with you."

He stared at me for a minute and then asked, "Can we talk about this later tonight, after dinner? I am really interested in what you said."

I agreed.

And then he said to me, "Hey, I'm going to sail the dhow over to a little village later today for something. Would you and your family like to sail there with me? There's a nice beach for the kids to play on."

Suzette and I had heard of a little village on the island, not far away on the island that was supposed to be cool, so we accepted his kind offer to sail us there.

Without us knowing, he took us to a different little village, and it was on the mainland, where police later told us that the terrorist group al-Shabaab was alive and well. We knew that witchcraft was strong there too, and then Omar pointed out the spot where some foreign tourists had recently been abducted, dragged deeper into Somalia and murdered. Of course, he didn't tell us this until we got on shore and started walking through the village.

He paraded our barefoot family through the village on the road that went directly to the political Somali border 20 miles away. The village was a dark place. Everyone was nervous, even Omar's brother, Ali. As we slowly wandered the sand streets of this remote African village, our captain would disappear now and then into a thatched roof hut or stop to talk quietly with one of the elders of the village. And they all stared at us.

We just tried to be friendly and waved and smiled to everybody. Smiles broke out most everytime we smiled big or said something in Swahili to the locals. If I said I was a bit uncomfortable, that would be like trying on my jeans from high school and saying that they were a tad uncomfortable. We needed to get out of there, and so I told

Omar we needed to leave right away. And that's what we did. The only reason I believe we didn't have trouble was because we had the kids with us. They LOVED seeing our children. I'm so glad my kids didn't have to witness me killing any terrorists.

Later that night, back at Mike's Camp, Omar and I talked for about 5 hours until after midnight about Allah, nature and the moon in the cloudless sky up above. We also talked about how a person can have strong supernatural peace and inexpressible joy and a deep love in their life that is beyond understanding, even during storms. I knew that if Omar were to ever start that close relationship with his creator, there would be a huge shake up in that region because everyone knew, respected and listened to him.

I finally said goodnight, got my shower with fire heated water coming out of the hanging bucket in our huge bathroom hut and then went to our hut and found the kids asleep and Suzette praying. We talked for a bit about my conversation with Omar, and then I fell asleep. She didn't.

After about 45 minutes, Suzette shook me hard awake and urgently said, "Something is wrong. We need to pray *right now*!" I opened my eyes and I kid you not, there was a thick blackness in the room like we had never experienced in our lives. No light whatsoever. It was dry season, so there hadn't been a single cloud in the sky the whole week and there was a full moon, yet we couldn't even see our hands in front of our faces nor the stars through the big glassless windows like before I went to sleep. We felt a heavy, thick evil presence all around us like never before.

We prayed and rebuked the spirits as best as we knew how and left no Christian phrase unused. "In Jesus' name, you leave now! You have no rights! Get away from us! In Jesus' name, I throw, cast, kick, punch, order you out of here!" We didn't have internet, but texting worked sometimes, so I sent texts to family and friends to PRAY NOW!!!

After about an hour, the dark, thick, black cloud left our hut and we could see the bright stars in the cloudless skies through the big, huge window openings again. And that wonderful peace returned.

I know this sounds like crazy talk to some, but I'm just telling you what happened. Surely there could be an explanation for all of the blackness, but there was a heaviness in our spirits and we sensed an unmistakably strong evil. I'm not a highly emotional sensationalist kind of guy, but I witnessed what I witnessed, and I'm happy I'm able to tell you this story today.

NOT AGAIN!

Back in January of 2017, I once again noticed something strange. We'd just had a great Christmas selling season and for the year had sold more pieces than ever, 88,000 wallets, briefcases, belts, duffle bags, desk pads and more. We had a huge following, cool designs, a reputation for high quality products and great customer service, but once more we had no money in the bank. Something was wrong again, but I couldn't figure out what.

In June, I asked both our CFO and our COO whether they thought Richard, our general manager at the factory, was stealing from us. Both answered me the same way. "You sound very paranoid, Dave. Richard is a good man. He's not stealing from you." I thought, *"Where was the money going, then?"*

Just a few days later, Suzette got a message on her Facebook page from a long time faithful employee at the factory to let us know that people we trusted at the factory were stealing from us in major ways. She didn't say who, but she said it was happening.

Right away, I flew down to the factory and started sniffing around for anything suspicious. First, I discovered that a lot of the final prototypes I'd approved had been stolen from the sacred Final Sample room. I immediately ordered Richard to call the police and report the theft. I figured at least the thieves would see the police come into the factory, get nervous and stop.

Two weeks later, I checked with Richard about what the police had found out, and he said he had hired a private investigator named Ernesto instead. I rolled my eyes and figured it was a lost cause; the investigator would catch the thief and then require a bribe from him to keep his mouth shut and report back to us that everything had checked out fine and there was nothing to see here.

So, I called one of my lawyer friends to see if he knew anything about this Ernesto guy and the lawyer had nothing but great things to say about him and said that he was known all around town for his honesty. Ernesto was a retired cop who had ended his career investigating corruption within the police and military around the country.

He spent the next 3 weeks investigating and interrogating almost everybody in the factory, our suppliers and former employees. He did an incredible job, far better than I had expected. Suzette and I flew down to meet with Richard and Ernesto for the big reveal of what Ernesto had found.

We sat in the conference room, across the table from Richard and Ernesto, and Ernesto started showing us the video testimonials and confessions of about 20 former and current employees. We couldn't believe what we were seeing and hearing. Even the employees were actually admitting to all of the wrong they had done with Richard.

Then Ernesto turned off the videos and spun his chair directly toward Richard and said, "And your wife is corrupt too. She is deeply involved in the theft."

Richard's jaw dropped open, his eyes got wide and he said, with his hands on his head, "What? No. Oh my God. I can't believe this. This is crazy." And then he broke down crying.

After about a minute, he composed himself and said, "Wait, I *can* believe it. I knew there was something going on with her, but I never knew it was this bad. It all makes sense now."

Over the next couple of minutes, Richard continued to throw his wife under the bus and then rolled the bus back and forth over her. We couldn't believe what he was saying about her. But it all made sense. Richard's wife, Jessica, was known at the factory as someone who adamantly opposed our mission and everything we wanted to do. She had even tried hard to keep our employees and their kids away from Centro NOE and the daycare. She controlled everybody, and everybody was afraid of her. Richard had hired her to control the factory's books. FYI, it's usually okay to have couples work for you, but one cannot report to the other.

After running through all the evidence against her and getting Richard to confirm his wife's involvement, Ernesto turned to Richard and said, "Richard, and they say you are corrupt too." He went on to show the evidence and testimonials he had collected against him too. It was shocking. The external auditors said we lost about $1,000,000 USD, but I don't want to bore you with the details. Let's just say that it all worked out fine in the end.

Meanwhile, I started asking around for anyone who could manage our factory, and that's how we found Lindel Townsley. He was an older gentleman, tall and lanky with a big smile, and he was loved by everybody. He had committed his life to living in China to develop businesses and orphanages. All of his children were born and raised there, but he also learned he had a knack for factory operations.

He had moved back to the States to become a university professor but was bored by teaching. Lindel and I talked about the situation with the factory, and he decided to move to Mexico right away. At the same time, we hired a man named Pedro to be his assistant and help him translate. Lindel immediately began to untangle the disaster and poured encouragement and support into the faithful ones who were left.

LION'S HEART ACADEMY

Back in June of 2017, Suzette surprised me. We had our first big graduation at the daycare and parents got up to tell their stories. One of the fathers shared his story about how he and his wife felt so good being at work, knowing their kids were in such a loving place. And then he started to cry. He talked about how sad he was that his son had to leave and go out into the big, cold world of regular school with the masses of kids and teachers who couldn't love and protect him the way he was loved and protected at Leoncito's Daycare. There wasn't a dry eye in the room.

Once everyone had finished saying their piece, Suzette grabbed the microphone and blurted out, "Don't worry! In August, we will have our private school open for them to continue on with us. And it won't just be any school, but it will be the best school in this city."

What? I stared at the side of her head in shock and bewilderment. Lesson to married people: With big decisions, you should talk to each other about it before you tell everyone something is going to happen.

Nevertheless, in August we were able to open Lion's Heart Academy inside of the daycare with 12 students using a fully English Christian homeschool curriculum. And when the kids graduate, they get a high school diploma from a high school in the United States. It was the same curriculum one of our Rwandan boys was going through, and even my own youth pastor graduated using the same curriculum back in the '80s.

We have a gorgeous library as the centerpiece of the school with hundreds of storybooks for all ages of kids and adults, from Nancy Drew and Hardy Boys to Louis L'Amour and *The Little Red Hen*. We want the kids falling in love with reading because studies show that reading helps kids develop strong neural pathways, which raises their thinking and ability to do math, science and connect with others.

I also brought 12 chess sets and left them at the school. There's no better game for teaching reasoning than chess.

The problem with public schools, in so many countries around the world, is their curriculum seems designed to create, or maintain, a working class who doesn't question or challenge the ideas they're taught. They just do what they're told. One African friend called it a "chalk and talk" education. The teacher writes on the chalkboard what the students are supposed to copy down and memorize for the test. That is not the kind of education we wanted to offer.

MEMENTO MORI IN LEATHER

I had recently gone to back to back funerals for 2 friends. Both men had dedicated their lives to serving others and hundreds, if not thousands, of lives were changed through them. The funeral of my mentor, Clark Blakeman, was a packed house of about 1,000 people mourning a man who died before his time. The other funeral was also for a great man, who had dedicated so much of his life as a missionary serving the hurting and the outcast in Brazil. Both funerals were filled with stories and testimonies of the people who were impacted by those men. It was sad, yet very honoring.

Clark had a beautiful natural wood casket. It seemed to be exactly the appropriate casket for the man Clark was. The other man had a typical looking metal composite casket with the typical funeral swirls along the sides.

The wise Israeli King, Solomon, once said,

> It is better to enter a house of mourning than a house of feasting, since death is the end of every man, and the living should take this to heart. Sorrow is better than laughter, for a sad countenance is good for the heart. The heart of the wise is in the house of mourning, but the heart of fools is in the house of pleasure. (Ecclesiastes 7:2–4 BSB). Never has a truer word been spoken.

The funerals got me thinking, *What will my funeral be like?* I wondered. *In particular, what will my casket look like?* That's when I got the idea that I needed to make my own cool leather coffin, the coolest coffin that has ever existed in the whole world.

Even though I was feeling just fine, you don't plant a garden when you're hungry, and you certainly don't design a coffin when you need it. You never know. The death rate in Texas is 100 percent, so I figured I'd better get going.

It took about 6 months to get the coffin just the way I wanted it and it came out cooler than I had imagined. I heard more than one funeral director tell me that it was the coolest and best looking coffin they had ever seen.

Now that my coffin was finished, I had to do something to get the word out. Once again, our filmmaker, Joe, and I burned through several cigars thinking about how to present it. As I researched death, the Latin phrase *memento mori* kept coming up, meaning, "Remember, you too shall die." The theme is found in art, literature and architecture throughout history. One story often retold is of a victorious Roman general who, after returning from war, paraded through the streets in his chariot, waving to the masses as they cheered his greatness. But he made sure to have a man riding with him who would regularly whisper to him, *memento mori*. Remember, you too shall die.

Who doesn't need a reminder of our mortality to keep us grounded? I have found that pride is a killer and takes down a lot more people than war does. So that got me thinking: Everybody should have a coffin whispering to them, *"Remember, you too shall die."* It would help them to prioritize the most important things in life first.

In the Book of Ecclesiastes, the wisest man who ever lived listed a lot of sad and worthless things he had seen, and one of them was when a man worked so hard all his life and never stopped to enjoy the fruit of his labor or the rewards that God gave him. King Solomon said it was a shame, because they worked so hard to make all of that money or accomplish all that they did, only to die and leave it to people who didn't deserve it or earn it, then those who got it all had a blast either squandering it or giving it away. And then, Solomon said, everybody forgets the dead man's name.

That framed the concept for the coffin to be a reminder of having a good work-life balance. But the term *work-life* had become cliché. I needed something to catch people's attention, just like our 100 Year Warranty, which is way more noteworthy than the "Lifetime Warranty." Combining *memento mori* and *work-life balance*, I came up with *work-death* balance. Yep, now *that* would get people's attention.

On Halloween week of 2017, we launched the "Work Death Balance" video and it appeared on national TV too. On Halloween, we were featured on the *CBS Morning Show* in Dallas / Fort Worth. Someone from *Texas Monthly* saw the story and, in turn, did their own story about the owners of this Texas leather company who live in tents. The calls, emails and sales came pouring in. Of course, none of that would have happened if I would have listened to the people who told me not to do it because it was too weird to design a coffin.

• THIRTEEN •

Toyota Meets Their Match

In October of 2017, I went to the Texas Auto Writers Association (TAWA) event outside of Austin, Texas, where the Texas journalist reviewers decided which vehicles were the best of the year. All of the car brands were represented, as well as a lot of their chief engineers and executives.

Everybody wants to win Texas Truck of the Year, because the rest of the world sees it as America's Truck. I once took the wife and kids to a remote African village near the Tanzanian border, way deep in the bush, where most of the villagers had just recently seen their first lightbulb and Westerner. Their "store" was a small, rough mud hut with a few wooden planks for shelves. They had bags of beans, rice, sorghum and, I'm not kidding, a can of *Texas Barbecue Chips*. When I'm anywhere in the world, regardless of how remote, and someone asks me where I'm from, I reply, "I'm from Texas." And they say, "Ahhh . . . America."

The night before the event, TAWA held a big dinner where 170 people stood up and introduced themselves, with their company and what they did. When it got to the Toyota tables, a man stood up and said, "Hi, my name is Allen Vaught, and I run Land Cruiser North America for Toyota" and then passed the mic.

As soon as I heard that, I stood up, walked straight across the room and knelt down next to his chair and said, "Hi, Allen. My name is Dave Munson and I'm a big Toyota Land Cruiser fan. I also own Saddleback Leather Company and we're the Toyota Land Cruiser of the leather bag world. Our bags are indestructible. You can bend 'em, but you can't break 'em. And one day, I'm going to have a Saddleback Leather Edition Toyota Land Cruiser."

He looked at me, smiled and said, "We don't make special editions of the Land Cruiser. We sell every single one we can make. But it's nice to meet you."

The next day I went over to the Toyota tent to mix it up a little more with the folks there, and Allen introduced me to a man named Mike Sweers. Mike was the chief engineer for the Toyota Tundra. He said, "Dave, we checked out your company online last night and it's pretty impressive. Nice stuff. And we love your story. Would you be interested in doing a Saddleback Edition Toyota Tundra?"

I looked at him and said, "Well, let me think about it for a sec." And about a second later I said, "Yes. I would. Absolutely!" And that started the ball rolling and rolling and rolling and rolling and rolling and rolling.

DEFINING A BRAND

A few months later, Mike and I were talking on the phone and he said, "You know, Dave, the more Toyota has dug into your brand, the more we realize Toyota has never come across a brand that aligns more with Toyota than Saddleback Leather does."

He put together a presentation for the higher ups in Japan and got the nod to start the project. No one could believe it got to the nod stage, because doing something like this was unheard of at Toyota.

Up to that point, all I knew about Toyota was that they were a rock solid, well oiled machine that made the longest lasting, most durable vehicles in the world. What I didn't know was the principles that Toyota was founded on aligned almost perfectly with Saddleback. I had never met a company that aligned more with my brand either.

What I also didn't know was that the CEO of Toyota had just publicly announced, "No more boring cars," and their slogan is "Let's Go Places." It made me think about my own brand. What did people think about when they heard our name or carried a Saddleback piece?

When I first started Saddleback Leather, it was just me, my dad and my sister, so it was easy to keep the brand true to self. But as I began to hire people to represent the brand in marketing or customer service, they had to guess what they thought the brand was, and they said some pretty cringey things.

My wife's sister, Tina, started by helping out in customer service and would write in her customer service emails stuff like, "Yo dude, wassup? Just chillin' here with my board on the beach. Hang 10!" She thought that was cool. I told her, "Tina, we hired you because we like who you are and know other people will like who you are too, so be yourself, not anybody else." Another gal we hired would say stuff like, "Yeehaw, partner. Howdy do? Just hangin' out on the ranch here in Texas punchin' dogies. How can I help ya?" That was weird. But since I hadn't defined our brand, our people started making up what they thought it was or what they thought it should be, and so did our customers.

It was time for me to define who Saddleback really was so we would be consistent in our marketing and public image. If we had a well defined brand, then when a graphic designer or photographer thought about puting something out to the public, it had to align with the Saddleback brand. It couldn't have pink bubblegum letters.

So, I put together a Google Doc and asked everyone in the company to help me understand what they thought our brand was about.

What was our style? Who were we? What vibe was I putting off? I did this not for them to define our brand, but I wanted to know what they *felt* it was. I asked them to just put in one or two word answers to some of the questions.

For example, I asked them, "Which movies represent Saddleback?" About half of customer service said, "A cowboy Western movie like John Wayne." That wasn't right. We were Clint Eastwood meets Indiana Jones, not John Wayne. We could be riding a horse, but not wearing a 10 gallon hat and roping cows. Nothing wrong with the Western cowboy rodeo world, but that wasn't our brand. I came up with some other movies and books that worked with our brand: *The Man from Snowy River*; *The Natural*; *African Queen*; *Allan Quatermain*; *Robinson Crusoe*; *Indiana Jones*; *The Good, the Bad and the Ugly* and *Field of Dreams*. That is how I developed this profile of the Saddleback brand:

What kind of food represents Saddleback? Peppered beefsteak, not ham; not a boiled hot dog, but a big beefy kind of burnt roasted sausage dog; not a banana cream pie, but a pecan pie; fresh fish; meatloaf; biscuits and sausage gravy.

What kind of music would be in a Saddleback movie or at a Saddleback event? Acoustic unplugged; classical guitar; cello; a little blues harmonica; Johnny Cash not Garth Brooks; Jack Johnson; John Mayer; Billie Holladay; Frank Sinatra.

What kind of beverage? Cold glass of milk; cold water from a glass bottle or canteen; black coffee; hot tea; fresh squeezed lemonade or orange juice; no alcohol, even though I enjoy a nice dark beer with friends every now and then.

What kind of animals? Large, friendly dogs; wild horses; crocodiles; birds of prey; highland cows; mountain sheep.

What kind of art? Sketches; Rembrandt; da Vinci; sculpture; blank canvas; old photos; weaving; Norman Rockwell.

Which colors? Forest green; moss; olive; tan; dark coffee brown; rust; gray stone.

Which kind of vehicles or modes of transportation? Wooden canoe; sailing ship; raft; old Royal Enfield or Indian motorcycle; Toyota Land Cruiser; suspension bridge; walking; rope swing.

Which kinds of plants or trees? Wildflowers; big, gnarly dead tree; pine; ocotillo cactus; mesquite; pecan; moss; sunflower; purple thistle flower; redwood; mahogany; hops.

Which kinds of footwear? World War I service boots; early turn of the century hiking boots; classic toe cap oxfords; wingtips; flip flops; warm sheepskin slippers, barefoot.

What kind of clothing? Wool sweater; vests and waist coats; Levi's jeans; canvas jacket; cargo pants and shorts; a well worn leather belt; linen; Harris Tweed; flannel.

Which actors, characters or historical figures? Abraham Lincoln; Indiana Jones; Allan Quatermain; Robert Redford; Chris Pratt; Thomas Edison; Teddy Roosevelt; Bear Grylls; Denzel Washington; Billy Graham.

What kind of sports? Baseball; chess; rowing; rugby; ultimate frisbee; racquetball; fencing, mountain biking; billiards; shooting; longbow archery; sailing.

Which books or authors? C. S. Lewis; *Calvin and Hobbes*; Ernest Hemingway; H. Rider Haggard; *Treasure Island*; The Bible; *The Count of Monte Cristo*; Cicero; *The Far Side*; Life Hack books; *Don Quixote*; The Harvard Classics; *The Rime of the Ancient Mariner*.

Which countries or landscapes? Sub Saharan Africa; London; Montenegro; Australia; Oregon; Texas; Spain; New Zealand; Moab; desert landscapes; forest in winter; vast mountainous wilderness; wide open spaces.

Which tools? Axe; anvil; rope; shears; toothpick; single shot rifle; single blade pocketknife; chisel; pulley; Leatherman multi tool.

Which hobbies? Exploring; cartography; camping; photography; reading; travel; learning languages; writing; painting; fishing; frisbee; hiking.

Which professions? Architect, fine woodworker, professor, writer, archeologist, forest ranger, bush pilot, traveling evangelist, photographer, painter.

I didn't stop there. I also listed personality and feeling words that describe the Saddleback lifestyle: curious, adventurous, innovative, confident, durable, authentic, classic, funny, humble, quality, relational, utility.

Personality:

What does our brand sell? Goodness, adventure, lifestyle, community, exclusivity, a life well lived, craftsmanship, family, conversation, story, honesty, virtue, perseverance, happiness.

Which emotions do customers experience with our brand or bags? Pride, confidence, surprise, inspiration, anticipation, happiness, belonging, accomplishment.

Which words describe our brand's personality? Warm, faithful, real, enduring, friendly, timeless.

What are our brand values? Helpfulness, truthfulness, humility, generosity, continuous improvement, faithfulness, tolerance, integrity, freedom, exploration, humor.

What do we promise? 100 year warranty; authenticity; quality; care for people.

There you go. These don't add up to a concrete marketing plan, but the exercise provided me with a loose set of ideas, images and concepts so that we all shared the same idea of what Saddleback is and what it means to be part of it. It got me thinking more about my brand and anytime you can do that, you're one step ahead.

FOUNDED ON PRINCIPLE

When I researched the Toyota brand, I learned a lot and loved the parallels. The original family name was *Toyoda*, spelled with a *D*, which means "fruitful rice paddy." In the early years, the Toyoda family manufactured looms and sewing machines, but in the late 1920s, Sakichi Toyoda gave the nod to his son, Kiichiro Toyoda, to start manufacturing cars. And that's where the current name *Toyota* came from.

Sakichi was a virtuous and principled man and he permanently left his mark on the company. He died in 1935 and immediately, Kiichiro and Risaburo Toyoda collected and arranged the principles Sakichi regularly taught and held so dear. They released them in a formal written statement called "The Five Main Principles of Toyoda." I listed with them the virtues these principles represent.

1. *Always be faithful to your duties, thereby contributing to the Company and to the overall good.* (Virtues: Faithfulness, Diligence, Commitment, Responsibility, Discipline, Dignity, Humility, Respect, Helpfulness, Reliability)
2. *Always be studious and creative, striving to stay ahead of the times.* (Virtues: Wisdom, Learning, Innovation, Creativity)
3. *Always be practical and avoid frivolousness.* (Virtues: Simplicity, Integrity, Honesty, Practicality, Frugality)
4. *Always strive to build a homelike atmosphere at work that is warm and friendly.* (Virtues: Friendliness, Caring, Trustworthiness, Generosity, Kindness, Tolerance, Graciousness, Love)
5. *Always have respect for spiritual matters and remember to be grateful at all times.* (Virtues: Tolerance, Acceptance, Respect, Honor, Peace, Unity, Humility, Thankfulness)

These 5 principles and corresponding virtues were not written by their PR team. They formally wrote out these principles to establish a solid foundation for building the business on. Apparently, they knew that if they wanted to be successful, more than just financially, they would need a North Star statement to guide them.

What I have personally experienced over the past several years, as I've worked with a lot of executives and key people within Toyota, is that these principles, and their accompanying virtues, are spoken of and acted out in every area I've been involved with. At first, I couldn't believe Toyota had been able to keep this principled company culture so strong through the years. Every single person I've met in the company has treated everyone else with respect and humility. They have humbly said, in many different ways, that no one person is superior to or more important than another; they just have different responsibilities.

This is why you will never hear or see a Toyota commercial comparing themselves to other car brands or talking about how superior they are. They basically just humbly say, "We try hard to make very safe and reliable vehicles, and we hope you like them." I guess it's why so many of the people I've privately talked with tell me that once someone in the auto industry finally gets a job at Toyota, they plan for it to be their last.

The more I read things like the Five Main Principles of Toyota and other internal documents on how to manage, the more I saw they seemed a lot like a people company cleverly disguised as a quality car business. Their 5 key principles could be summarized as Humility, Respect, Integrity, Generosity and Continuous Improvement, and those principles showed up everywhere. Every year, the Japanese leadership even pray together for the safety of the people who buy their cars.

THE HAIR ON THE BACK OF MY NECK STANDS UP

In January of 2019, Saddleback Leather was looking and feeling great. We'd ended the year with unusually strong sales, had profit in the bank and the stress was off. The culture at the factory was much closer to the way we'd always wanted it, and our hope in the US economy was strong. And then I got an email from a man named Marcus Umlauff.

Marcus was the general manager of Toyota's Trucks and SUVs and he wanted to drive to my office to meet with me. I couldn't believe it. Was it finally actually happening after 2 long years of waiting? In the beginning of February, Marcus came into my office and we laughed and talked for about 3 hours. He learned more about me, and I learned a lot more about Toyota. He said Toyota had never done anything like this before, so if they were going to do a Saddleback Leather Edition Tundra, it had to be *very* special. It couldn't just have their normal leather on the inside with a Saddleback Leather badge slapped on the fender. He wanted something off the charts remarkable.

I suggested they not do an actual Saddleback Leather Edition Tundra, but rather offer a Saddleback Leather interior for all vehicles. He liked the idea, but Toyota decided to stick with the plan to make just 1500 special Saddleback Leather Limited Edition Tundras. They would soon be launching the Capstone edition Tundra, which was their posh, most luxurious edition. The Saddleback Leather Edition was going to have the slightly lifted and more aggressive extreme offroad package combined with the extreme luxury of the Capstone Edition, but it was going to have the most durable and coolest leather seats in the world, at least that was my goal.

I told Marcus I had only designed a couple of auto interiors for my own Land Cruiser and our old Land Rover Defender, but felt confident I could design the seats and interior to the level of the truck or beyond. I walked Marcus to the front door, gave him a hug goodbye and went back to my office in shock. I couldn't believe what had just happened. The Toyota project had come back to life. Then COVID happened and everything came screeching to a halt.

In March of 2021, Marcus started the Saddleback Leather Edition Tundra project back up and I got busy. Of course, as usual, I prayed that God would help these seats turn out to be the coolest, longest lasting seats that have ever existed and that somehow He would get more glory from them than He had ever gotten from any other automotive interior in history. As I like to say, it never hurts to ask.

GETTING IT RIGHT

I started working with the German tannery Bader to design leather with just the right look and feel to match Saddleback's brand. The normal thickness of automotive leather is 0.9–1.3 mm, but Saddleback's leather is 2–2.2 mm, and I felt their thinner leather would be bad for my brand. So, I told Christoph Murrer, the Austrian chemist and leather scientist at Bader, that I needed the leather for the Tundra to be at our thickness, but he slowly shook his head no and laughed. "Dave," he said, "they told me to do whatever you ask, since this is a really special project, but nobody uses leather that thick. In fact, I've never even heard of a company asking for it before. It certainly wouldn't pass Toyota's stringent standards for suppleness, so it wouldn't be comfortable. Why would you want it like that? Let me show you some nice 1.3–1.5 mm leather. That would be good enough and still be thicker than 95 percent of what is used for cars around the world."

It was my turn to shake my head. "Oh, Christoph, come on. You're a really smart guy. If there's anybody in the world who could figure out how to create the thickest automotive leather ever in existence, and make it comfortable to sit on, it would be you. I know how bad Bader wants to get their foot in the door with Toyota as a leather supplier. Will you at least give it a shot? In fact, I insist."

Three weeks later, Christoph asked me to come by the tannery, which is actually only about 5 minutes away from our factory in Leon, to show me the results. You should have seen him. He had the biggest smile on his face as he laid out the full hide of 2 mm thick leather. His team had figured out how to make it thick enough *and* achieve the suppleness required for comfort by Toyota. Even they couldn't believe they had actually figured it out.

I congratulated them, but then brought up another problem for them to solve. "The color matched Saddleback's, but that was it," I said. With our bags, there is no question in people's minds that they are made out of leather. Our leather has tons of veins and stretch marks and varied high and low tones that give it a lot of natural character. This hide looked like someone spread peanut butter perfectly and evenly all over it. I told him it wouldn't work and that it needed more character.

Christoph looked at me, shook his head again and said, "Dave, everybody asks for natural looking leather with character, but it's simply impossible to have that and still pass all of the federal regulations and, at the same time, the color not stain or discolor or rub off onto people's clothes. And, Toyota requires it to stay the same color for at least 10 years. Let me show you a leather we made for BMW that simulates character with a cloudy spraying technique we engineered."

He showed it to me and right away, a little vomit came up in the bottom of my throat, but I caught it and swallowed it back down.

"Christoph, listen, you're an Austrian and you work for a company of German leather engineers. If there's anybody in the world who could give me leather with character, it's you. I have all of the confidence in the world that you're smart enough to figure it out. I insist."

Again, about 3 weeks later, I came back into the tannery, and they proudly showed me the results, and it was kind of better but was nothing to write home about.

They were proud they had gotten so far with a new technique they had never tried before and were excited to keep on trying. The thing was, they had never *had to* figure it out. They never had a constraint. They always just said it was impossible, and sold the automaker something bland looking. But this time, it was really important that they figure it out because the window to get into Toyota was closing, and I wouldn't take "good enough" for an answer. I wanted great.

About a month after that, I was up in Detroit at Bader's North American headquarters when the next leather sample arrived. We laid the roll on the table and unrolled the hide, and that's when the trumpets started sounding from above and a heavenly choir started singing all around. It was so gorgeous. The tones varied from high to low and there was a lot of natural marbling throughout. Everyone around the table was smiling and laughing and high fiving. It was the coolest automotive leather anyone had ever seen in their decades of experience, and right away they said it would be an industry changer.

DESIGNING THE SEATS

At the same time the leather was being developed, Cristian Farcas of Toyota's design group was assigned to me to work with me to design the interior seats, dashboard and other surfaces of the Limited Edition Tundra. I flew up to Toyota's design headquarters in Detroit and started working shoulder to shoulder with Cristian, using their realistic 3D software to get just the right look to the seats and the rest of the interior. What a blessing it was to team up with Cristian, who helped me understand a lot more about designing automotive seats and suggested some great details I wouldn't have thought of on my own.

You know how in log cabins when the floor, walls, doors, ceilings and tables are all made out of the same wood, it can be too much wood? Well, that can also happen with too much leather in a truck. The seats had to have a lot of leather but not too much and it took quite a while to figure out just the right balance.

Cristian and I also had to determine the perfect stitch count per inch, with just the right thickness and color of thread in just the right places to give it the level of rough texture it needed for the size of the seats. It had double stitching in some places but not all. Too much or too little would have messed it up. I also needed it to be simple and plain, without unnecessary layers and lines, because I wanted the heavy character of the leather to be what inspired awe rather than creative lines and shapes. I felt the entire interior of the truck would become too busy if we overdesigned the seats. The design of the dashboard and doors were already complex enough, and we didn't need complex seats competing with them, but rather enhancing them.

Cristian suggested we try out Saddleback's crested seams on the seats and I loved the idea. The seams exposed the edges of the leather to show the thickness and it looked GREAT on the seats. But I only wanted it in 3 places as texture accents on some sections of the seats so it wouldn't be too much. He laughed and said, "I'm not even allowed to think like this, but let's see how we can do it and if they'll even allow these seams."

Apparently, it had never been done before in automotive, but on my bags, it's one of our consistent design features across all that I do, so it made sense to include the crested seams in the truck seats too.

The exact right amount of leather, combined with using the perfect kind of leather on a simple seat design, made the final product come out cooler than I ever could have imagined. In fact, when we all saw the final sample of the seat at Toyota's design headquarters, no one could believe it. You should have heard how many Toyota employees told me they even wanted those seats in their own cars. Maybe I'm a little partial to my own design, but I've never seen a car interior that I've liked more.

MIRACLE AT TOYOTA

Some longtime Toyota employees later told me that within Toyota, this Tundra project was considered a miracle because nobody believed it could happen. Actually, one person told me that the heart of the Saddleback Leather Edition Tundra project had stopped 3 times along the way, but all 3 times the project got defibrillator paddles to the chest and was jolted back to life.

Because of all of the prayer that went into this project, it's obvious to me that God did His Jedi Total Mind Control trick on all of us, from the design to the engineering to the manufacturing to the launch video. He put it in the hearts of the general manager, Marcus Umlauff, and the chief engineer, Mike Sweers, to push it through, and God had developed and honed their leadership skills over the years to masterfully navigate the project through all of the different departments, divisions and naysayers at Toyota. How it worked out was nothing short of a miracle.

One of the guys at Toyota told me he was on a business trip with one of the naysayers who wanted to shut the project down. The man said Saddleback was too small of a company, too little known and the whole thing was a bad idea. As they were getting off the plane, a stranger in front of them had a Saddleback Leather briefcase and the guy who was for the project asked the man, "Excuse me, is that a Saddleback Leather bag?" The man turned to them and excitedly went on a rant about how great it was and how he got compliments on it all the time and how everybody at his office owned one too. The Toyota executives both laughed, and the naysayer said *nay* no longer.

More than one high level employee told me that, as a whole, Toyota loved all that they had learned and how they had improved because of doing this special little project. They said it forced them to innovate, speed up unnecessarily long processes and think differently about parts of their business because they were forced to get this special project through in a short time and with special providers. Not only that, but I believe it raised the bar on their own quality. It used to be that the mechanics of their vehicles lasted longer than any interior ever could, but that definitely changed with this leather project. There was a lot of pain and stretching, but everyone loved the result.

· FOURTEEN ·

The Life Altering Gift

When Cross was 8 years old, one afternoon he drew out 20 different shapes of bags that he thought would be cool to have. I didn't ask him to do it; he just wanted to design them. When I walked in the door, he ran up and handed me his stack of papers and waited for me to give him my opinion. I took the stack of papers, sat down in my chair and looked through them. I was amazed.

"Cross, can you see these bags in your head all finished?"

"Yes," he said.

"Can you spin these bags around in your head and see the backs and bottoms and stuff like that?"

Again, he replied, "Yes."

I turned to Suzette and said in a deep and excited tone, "Well, it looks like we have a bona fide designer on our hands."

Over the next couple of years, Cross wasn't too enthused to follow through with his designs because he was just a kid. But when he hit 10, he started to get into it. My Saddleback Leather bags were too heavy for him to personally carry since he had such a small frame, so I told him it was time he designed a lightweight backpack for himself.

It could be made out of pigskin leather, which was lightweight and thinner, but also tougher than the cowskin.

As he designed his bag, we sat together and I walked him through the design process. We talked about the importance of reinforcing stress points and different ways to do it. I showed him the finer details of designing with triangles, thirds and just the right proportions so the visual weight of the design was pleasing to the eye. We talked about stitching, edges and having a consistent theme to the bags so they looked intentional or "designed." Over the next several months, his backpack was taking shape and before we knew it, he had his first Hogsback Backpack. Now it was time for him to field test it.

WIENER-KICKING ELEPHANTS

In the summer of 2019, we headed out again to Rwanda to see our boys and then flew with about a dozen of them to the neighboring country of Uganda. We wanted to raise their ceilings and knew that an airplane flight should do the trick. They couldn't believe that they were actually on an airplane and soon realized that if that were true, then what else could be true? We landed in Kampala and headed to the city of Jinja, where we would vacation with them at the head of the River Nile and on the massive Lake Victoria. I got a cool video describing the Front Pocket Backpack alone on an island at the source of the Nile bubbling out of the ground. All of the boys later agreed that flying on an airplane helped them to understand that they were capable of greater things than they had ever imagined.

A day after we got back to Rwanda from Uganda, we took a couple more flights heading west to the pristine, unadulterated country called Gabon. I had read about their world's largest leatherback turtle migration, but the few tourist videos we could find were all in French and hard to figure out.

We soon learned why tourists weren't welcome. The French government had colonized many resource rich countries of Africa, gave them borders and ruled them with an iron fist, and then legally gave them back their independence in the 1960s while continuing to rule indirectly to continue getting all of their natural resources. The former president of France, Jacques Chirac, once said that 60 percent of France's income came from Africa.

France obviously taught the Gabonese to only speak French, which meant they could only ever interact with France or the other poor former French colonies. They pretty much made it impossible for Gabon to interact with anyone who didn't speak French, and France fought tooth and nail to keep everybody out of that oil rich country. In fact, back in 2016, we had applied for a tourist visa to Gabon, but they insisted we show them our bank statements and a formal letter from someone inviting us. I thought they were going to ask for a letter from my mother next.

In 2017, the president of Gabon, Ali Bongo, opened the country up for the Africa Cup of Nations soccer finals and created an online visa system for visitors. So now we had a way in.

Gabon is a super peaceful country on the west coast of Central Africa with a heavy population of lowland gorillas and abundant wildlife like we had never seen before. In fact, the most recent Tarzan movie was filmed there. We only knew a little French when we arrived, but we learned quite a bit over the next 10 days. It was so beautiful and definitely one of our favorite trips ever.

Gabon certainly wasn't fancy, and places to stay were few and far between because tourism wasn't hardly a thing until two years earlier. But it was loaded with cool things to do at very low prices. We missed the giant Leatherback Turtle migration when 30,000 of them come up on shore to lay eggs October through December. And we missed the turtle hatch, which happens from January through March. Nor did we see any of their chimpanzees, black panthers or surfing hippos. We were also too early for the big crocodile hatch in December.

But we did see a lot of non-surfing hippos, the ridiculously active humpback whale migration just offshore, maybe 75 elephants and a lagoon island packed with nesting storks and pelicans. We went gorilla trekking and did a little of their world class game fishing too. Suzette and I didn't catch anything, but the kids caught some big barracudas almost as long as they were.

It was in Gabon where Cross launched his new Hogsback Collection with an epic video of his favorite backpack with an elephant right behind him kicking his own wiener. We also filmed highlight videos of the leather chess set, Suzette's Love 41 Wanderers Backpack with the gorillas and more.

If you ever visit Gabon, be sure to stay at Loango National Park, and also stay at the Hotel La Baie des Tortues Luth to see the Leatherback Turtle migration. And tell the owner, Abbad, that Dave and Suzette said hi.

PEDRO TAKES OVER

In 2018, after a year of Lindel Townsley traveling back and forth twice a month from Leon to Arkansas, he told me, "Dave, all of my life I wanted to grow old with my wife, but now I realize we're growing apart. I've enjoyed it here, but I need to get back to my wife." He told me things at the factory were stable and fairly cleaned up and he thought his assistant, Pedro, could help run the place until I found someone new.

We immediately started looking for Lindel's replacement, and a friend of ours, Steve Hackett, who was running a group of factories and companies, said he would help us with the interviewing process. He coached me on what to look for and gave me some good questions to ask. Soon, we found Denny Garcia, and Steve said he was a deal at twice the price.

Five months later, a big factory in Houston offered him twice the price and he left. He moved there about 3 days before everything shut down for COVID.

Pedro was going to have to do the job during COVID, but little did we know his understanding of how to run a business, much less a factory, was not nearly where it needed to be, and the business started getting messy.

AND THEN . . . COVID

In late January of 2020, we were in Rwanda and planning to spend some time in Italy on the way back. A friend of mine there, Mauro, was famous for designing and building custom seats for Ferrari, so I thought I could learn a thing or two from him as I was preparing to design seats for the Toyota Tundra. I was also going to visit a few famous tanneries and get inspiration in the leather markets of Florence.

I had big plans, but there was a rumor going around about something called a coronavirus in Italy, and they were discouraging people from traveling there. Luckily, we were able to cancel our hotel and car reservations and reroute for a long layover in England until the COVID thing blew over. I did a nice little demo video for the new Big Mouth Backpack at Stonehenge to take up some time, but we were soon told to get back to the US or stay in England for a long time. We got one of the last flights out. Shortly after getting home, everything shut down, which sure threw a kink in our business.

On March 22nd, 2020, both President Trump and Governor Abbott of Texas put out the word looking for any manufacturer who was able to consider pivoting their work to make personal protective equipment (PPE) for the medical field to protect doctors and first responders working with COVID patients.

I immediately looked up what PPE included, which was masks, isolation gowns, head and shoe coverings and so on, basically, anything that keeps germs off of first responders.

I thought, *If we can sew thick, high quality leather, then for sure we can sew some high quality PPE.* I brought the idea up to Suzette and she immediately agreed that we should stop making leather goods and try to help the situation by making PPE.

Right away, I went to a medical supply store and bought some PPE samples and took them to our factory in Mexico. We put all leather production on hold, bought some lighter weight sewing machines for textiles and moved completely over to cutting and sewing fabric. But, of course, I wasn't about to make crap PPE. I wanted it to be the longest lasting, most comfortable, healthiest and most environmentally friendly PPE in the world.

So, we went 100 percent cotton, which is very breathable, comfortable and reusable up to at least 100 washes before it needs to be easily waterproofed again. And when cotton goes into the landfill, it decomposes and turns back into dirt in a matter of months.

PPE made from polyester is about 10 percent the price of cotton, but it causes contact allergy rashes, lets off 500,000 microplastic particles with every wash that coats the ocean floor and takes 200 years to decompose in landfills. Polyester also lets bacteria breed on it so it stinks after only a few washes and everyone who wears polyester gets hot and sweaty because it doesn't breathe. And polyester in your sheets makes people toss and turn in their sleep because it traps the body's vapors under the covers instead of absorbing in and evaporating out of the cotton all night.

It took about 3 weeks to ramp up before we were producing face masks and isolation gowns. I knew the window to manufacture and sell them wouldn't be open very long before the floodgates of China opened and low quality, single use polyester landfill gowns would flood in. So, we got right to work and sewed thousands upon thousands of high quality, reusable and breathable cotton isolation gowns for the medical field. I looked extensively online and couldn't find any nicer or higher quality ones than ours.

Little did we know that in April of 2020, almost the whole world would shut down for COVID and all factories in Mexico would be forced to close. In Leon, our factory was the only one with the light on since we were considered an essential business, because we were providing equipment for the medical world to do their job. In no time at all, we had a line down the street of people looking for work and had about 500 people employed around the clock. It wasn't pretty, but we helped our employees provide for their families and neighbors and we stayed in business.

RESCUED BY OUR SADDLEBACK COMMUNITY

In May 2020, I saw a report of the top 100 booming and the bottom worst tanking products on Amazon. The booming things were things like breadmaking machines, garden gloves and external monitors. The two worst selling things on the list were luggage for travel and briefcases for going to business meetings. Those were our number 1 and number 2 product lines that put bread on our table. It wasn't looking good for us, and even though we were selling PPE, we weren't sure how we were going to survive.

I immediately started heavily promoting our antimicrobial leather home office designs that viruses couldn't live on, like our desk pads, mouse pads and catchall valet trays. We sold all we had, but it wasn't enough.

But then something very cool started happening. We saw some posts on Saddleback fan groups saying, "Hey, I know Saddleback has to be hurting right now. I'm going to buy something even though I don't really need it. They're always supporting so many people, it's time for people to support them."

Others jumped onboard too, and our sales went up. Thank you, Cary Okawa, James Roberson, David Pope, Jimmy Nelson, Agni and so many more, too many to list. Very cool of you.

MY FIRST QUALITY BOOTS

I told a friend of mine, who is well known and highly respected in the shoe and boot industry, that my British American friend, Julian Imrie, is helping me design some boots. He said, "You know Julian Imrie? That man stands tall in the boot world. I first saw his work in Japan in around 2008, and it changed the industry." Why he said that about Julian was because back in the early 2000s, he couldn't find a pair of old fashioned boots like something his grandfather would have worn, so he designed and sculpted a pair for himself. Ralph Lauren took notice and asked him to design some boots for them too. Julian ended up making shoes and boots for the Who's Who of Hollywood. When he is at Steven Spielberg's parties, he introduces Julian as "My shoemaker, Julian Imrie."

Julian was designing shoes and living in a little motel in Leon, Guanajuato, when COVID hit, so I invited him to stay in our company home by the factory to ride out the pandemic. We only went down to Mexico a couple times a month, and I hated that the house was empty so much of the time, so he moved in.

Shortly after moving in, Julian asked if he could trace my foot on a piece of paper. He said it was for if one day he should want to make some boots for me.

"Sure," I replied and stood on the paper.

A few months later, he proudly pulled out a pair of really cool looking lace up ankle high Service boots for me to try on. I had no idea how my life was about to change.

Right away, I said, "Wow, I love these things! They are easily the nicest pair of boots I have ever owned. Can you explain to me what the difference is between these $700 boots and, let's say, a pair of boots that look just like them but are priced at $300?"

Julian went on to lay it out and I couldn't believe what I was learning. Up to that point, I had always thought expensive shoes were all just marketing and status symbols but they weren't really worth the extra cost. He explained to me that his boots are made using about $120 to $150 of all natural quality materials as opposed to about $29 of leather and synthetic material used to construct a $300 boot. He said high quality boots will last about 3 times longer and look newer for decades as opposed to the $300 boots that flatten out, lose their shape and look like dumpy 50 year old boots after just a few years. He said the shape of his boots is orthopedic, so it's time consuming and expensive to shape the leather around the form (last) of the shoe. But hand lasting gives a far superior long term quality result.

And because of the anatomically correct shape, the feet pretty much think they're walking barefoot and that lets the arch and other foot and ankle muscles exercise and get strong again. If the toe bones stay in a straight line with the rest of the foot bones, then the ligaments, muscles and tendons in the foot will not stretch out and get weak. If the big toe gets gently pushed toward the second toe, that eventually deforms the toes and is the main cause of most, if not all, foot, ankle, shin, knee, hip and lower back pain. That and cushioned shoes.

Made sense to me, so I wore the shoes and got a lot of compliments on them, which was the first time in my life someone complimented me on my shoes. But then I fell deeply in love with them. I had had consistent knee pain (patellar tendonitis) and foot pain (plantar fasciitis) for at least 15 years, and it all went away permanently after wearing Julian's boots for about 3 months. And, my second biggest toe was longer than my big toe for years (clubbed toe), but when my toes got back in alignment with the bones and my arch got strong and healthy again, my toes went back to their normal length too.

Julian chose this last and slightly modified it to be even more handsome because it was good looking and was anatomically correct, but he didn't realize all of the immense health benefits it provided.

So, now I'm wearing these classy, high quality, good looking expensive boots, but didn't have a lot of clothes to wear with such a high level lace-up boot. They didn't go very well with cargo shorts nor with my Northwest outdoors mountaineering style, so I needed to dress more gentlemanly if I wanted to wear Julian's amazing boots. Suzette, who is highly skilled in the art of looking good, so she started buying me waist coats, higher quality dress shirts and various Harris Tweed jackets to go with my new great looking footwear. My style was definitely maturing.

Because I was wearing those boots, I was dressing nicer almost every day, which gave me a little extra skip in my step, which made me raise my chin just a tad higher, which made me feel like a million bucks, which helped me to lead the Saddleback team in more of a dignified and professional way. I guess you could say I was dressing for success. They are the highest quality, longest lasting boots I've ever put my feet in.

So, I thought to myself, *If other people experienced what I am experiencing, then it would help them too. I need to offer high quality boots and shoes like these at Saddleback too.* You see, I won't design or sell just anything. I have to need it, think it's cool or it has to have helped me personally. For example, I don't make fanny packs, for obvious reasons, nor Apple watch straps. Why would I want a distracting little computer on my wrist?

But I did make a cool leather case for my amazing Light Phone II, since it changed my life when I switched over to it from my stupid iPhone that was destroying my life. By the way, they say if you want to fix the problem of screentime with kids, just fix the problem of screentime with parents. I taught my kids that discipline doesn't need to sit on the edge of temptation. I wasn't disciplined enough to stay off of my iPhone, so I now mainly only use it for international travel or getting into Texas Rangers baseball games. I'm too busy and I have too much important and creative work to do to have a constantly distracting and memory destroying smartphone in my pocket. My brother now works at Microsoft and he made the switch to the Light Phone and said it changed his life so much that he could never go back to a smartphone again.

The idea of designing and selling boots and shoes that could change and help people like they helped me was so exciting, but even more so when I learned the unbelievably strange and cool twist to the story. I had no idea what was involved in designing high quality boots, but there's more than I had ever imagined.

I designed boots with Julian and learned that a boot is not truly a quality boot unless it has these 4 components. It has to be made with quality materials, made with quality construction, have a quality shape and have a quality design. Who cares if the materials are great, if it falls apart because of shabby construction? Who cares if they stay together for decades, but they aren't shaped anatomically correct and cause all kinds of foot, knee, hip or lower back pain? And who cares if it is quality in all 3 of those areas, if you have to set your dignity aside by wearing the equivalent of a fanny pack or headgear on your feet? So, Julian, Mr. GQ himself, and I designed what we feel are some of the all around highest quality shoes and boots in the world.

This is cool, but it gets cooler. A cool thing I learned after we got going on the designs is that the last that we are using to shape the boots around has had more boots made on it than any other boot or shoe in the history of the world. For 58 years, this last was used exclusively by all branches of the military from 1912 to about 1970. Every single American soldier you'll ever see in old war footage was wearing boots made on one of the 6 generations of this orthopedic last. And we are using the classier, more orthopedic second generation of this historical and biomechanically amazing last. The newer generations of the last are a little too clunky looking for my taste.

Here's where the story gets even cooler. I found out, after we were already designing the boots on this last, that it's called the Munson Last. My name is Dave Munson. But wait, there's more. Between 1908 and 1912, Dr. Edward Lyman Munson, and the Shoe Board he assembled, perfected this last by studying the feet of 2,000 soldiers and fitting them with thousands of different boots as experiments. They ordered the soldiers to march 8 miles, rest 24 hours and then march the 8 miles right back. The Shoe Board found that 38% of their soldiers had big foot problems and many of whom couldn't even finish the march in their current military boots. Dr. Munson said that the boots made with the Munson Last fixed 100% of their foot problems.

So, I did the Ancestry DNA test and found that Dr. Munson and I share a common grandfather from New Haven, Connecticut, and now I am carrying on his work for the Munson family. In 1912, Munson published his book explaining all of the science and data in depth called *The Soldier's Foot and the Military Shoe*. Expect to see a lot more about this in the coming years because it was such a life changer.

WHAT TO DO FOR THE REST OF MY LIFE?

My birthday is on June 21st, which is the longest day of the year and the first day of summer, also known as the Summer Solstice. Suzette's birthday is the opposite. It's on December 20th, which is sometimes the shortest day of the year and the first day of winter, also known as the Winter Solstice. It has been said that we are *solar opposites*.

And since I was turning 50 in 2021, what better way to spend my 50th birthday than to be in Mexico in the middle of another long family business roadtrip. We left Fort Worth in our 2006 Toyota Tundra, with our 3 Labrador Retrievers in the back, and drove the

1,000 mile journey and, of course, stopped in the old and gorgeous mountain town of Real de Catorce, kind of along the way. We stayed in Leon for a couple of weeks and then flew from there to Southeastern Europe to drive and explore for a few more weeks.

We rented a car in Zagreb, Croatia, and drove down through the beautiful countryside, and did a video describing our Medium Bifold Wallet in Plitvice Lakes National Park. We then drove to Dubrovnik and did a nice video demonstration of our upcoming 15" Grandfather Hard Briefcase. From there, we drove to the country of Montenegro and stayed for a few more days to film our Tow Belt and the 13" Grandfather Hard Case above the gorgeous walled city of Kotor.

We headed northeast from Montenegro to Bosnia and Herzegovina (it's one country, but you have to say both names together). The road signs were all in Russian, so that was brutal, but since the Russian language has a lot of Greek letters in it, I was generally able to sound them out. Remember, ancient Greek was my minor in college, and this was the first time I'd actually been able to use it for anything other than minor Bible translation. It made me smile.

In Mostar, there is a very famous old bridge over the river named Stari Most, and I did a nice video beneath it describing the 10" Grandfather Hard Case. And in all of these places, Cross was my trusty drone pilot for better scenic effects.

We drove back to Zagreb and then flew to Mexico, where we made a couple of small design changes to those products that I found were needed, and then drove the 1,000 miles back to Texas. It was some roadtrip and a great way to kick off my second 50 years of life. Now the real fun was about to begin.

Back to 2009, I was invited by a friend to have lunch with a man named Zig Ziglar, right before he died. He was about 82 years old and was widely considered to be one of the most successful men of his generation. There were only 6 of us at lunch and I sat right across the table from him. For the first 10 minutes of the lunch, Zig went on about how amazing his wife, the "Redhead," was. And then he went on for the next hour and a half imparting wisdom to us.

So, near the end of our lunch I asked him, "Zig, if all of your books, courses and talks were to disappear off the face of the earth and you could only leave us with one book, what would you write about?"

Right away he said, "Number one, Court Your Spouse because success starts at home. Number 2, Encourage People. And number 3, Help Everyone Around You to be as successful as they can be, and then you'll have everything you ever wanted or dreamed of."

It struck me that all 3 of those things were outwardly others focused: Love others, encourage others, help others. So, for these to work, it was required that we be genuinely interested in other people. In other words, to think about the self of others more than the self of me. In other words, the key to success was to be humble. That seemed especially relevant as I faced the rest of my life.

He also told us his story. He said when he was 47, he was unemployed and in debt, but at 48, he wrote his bestselling book *See You at the Top*, and that's when things started to click. Rick Warren wrote *The Purpose Driven Life* at around the age of 50.

I met a very successful man who said he had done a lot of significant things in life, but he said his impact only started going *deep and wide* at around the age of 50. The leaders in Jesus' time were surprised by the wisdom and authority he demonstrated when he spoke, because they believed you have nothing important to say until you're 50. It's widely known that 50 to 60 are your money earning years. Those years are when you often pay things off and earn your retirement.

It turns out we're all in training until we're 50. By then, hopefully, you've made some major mistakes and gained some wisdom. And now you're better at deciding what to do and what not to do next, even though you never stop making mistakes and learning. Until then, get all of the experience and training you can get. Move to other countries, try new things and learn as much as you can. King Solomon was the wisest man who ever lived, and he said, over and over again, we should seek wisdom and knowledge and understanding because those things are more valuable than silver and gold and precious stones.

Driving on another family business road trip, this time through Italy, we got an Airbnb in Rome overlooking the great Roman Colosseum. Of course, the second night there we watched *The Gladiator* with the TV in front of us and the lit up Colosseum out the window behind it. And that made me think of something I'd read by Cicero. Perhaps he'd written the words 2,100 years ago, sitting in the exact spot where I was looking out my window, though the Colosseum hadn't been built then. In his Treatise *On Old Age*, he said, "Neither white hair nor wrinkles can at once claim influence in themselves. It is honorable conduct of earlier days that is rewarded by possessing influence at the last." I hope this encourages you as it did me.

Turning 50 might not be so bad.

OFFICIAL LEATHER GOODS OF THE TEXAS RANGERS

Earlier in 2021, the Fort Worth Hispanic Chamber of Commerce heard about our work with the kids at our school in Mexico, and so gave us an honorary membership. We then had one of their gatherings at our headquarters, and at that gathering we told them we were doing a book drive for our school in Mexico because we believe one of the keys to a successful education is getting people using their imagination through reading. We were creating a library full of fun English-language storybooks, hoping to develop in them a lifelong love for reading, but we needed books.

It just so happened that Stephanie Gaytan from the Texas Rangers was there and thought we would be a great fit to work with The Texas Rangers Foundation, which helps kids who need a hand up in the Dallas, Fort Worth area.

In early November of 2021, we decided to partner with the Texas Rangers Major League Baseball team as The Official Leather Goods of the Texas Rangers, just a few days after they finished 60-102 for their fifth consecutive losing season, and most losses in their 61 year history. Still, we knew it would work out for us, and we worked hard at being a blessing to them.

In November of 2023, two seasons after we lost 102 games, the Rangers made the playoffs and then broke an all professional sports record with 11 straight playoff wins on the R-O-A-D against the Rays, Orioles, Astros and Diamondbacks. And they won the World Series for the first time! Boy, has that been fun!

So, obviously, I was wondering how we could get our leather bags stamped with "World Series Champions Texas Rangers" on the front. Millions of Texas Rangers fans would be excited to own some piece of Rangers history, something more than just a t-shirt, hat or a yard sign. So, I reached out to the most amazing Chad Wynn at the Rangers and asked if he would connect me with the right person to talk to at the Major League Baseball headquarters to see about licensing.

The licensing people at MLB knew who we were, and right away they fast tracked us to the decision maker. They were actually excited to get us going, but they had one requirement: They said we could work with the Rangers, but we had to work with the 29 other teams too. They said it was perfect timing, since so many clubs had been asking for higher quality goods to sell and they thought we would be a homerun.

LIKE MY GRANDFATHER'S BUT BETTER

To start 2022, we launched a yearlong campaign of *The Grandfather Collection*. I designed 12 different old fashioned looking cases, like our grandfathers would have carried. They were not designed for fancy kings and princes but rather for the common man, the plowman or the stonemason who had business to take care of. They were a combination of cool rugged leather with unfinished edges, yet refined with handstitched corners and a clean, simple look.

I would have launched cases like that sooner, but my first 11 attempts over the years were just not right. They were either too heavy or just a little weird looking. When we stick with something for long enough, we mature and get better at doing that thing. The thing I stuck with was designing leather bags and cases, and so this design had to eventually be figured out. When I finally saw the finished cases, I absolutely loved them. They were lightweight, looked exactly the way I had always imagined and they were tough.

After one solid year of marketing them, we were rewarded by the American Advertising Federation with a gold award for Best eCommerce Campaign. Here's what we did.

Each month, we released a different Grandfather Case. And for each, I imagined an era appropriate scene of a grandfather using or carrying that specific case or tray. I then had our in house artist, Salvador, paint that setting. We numbered each of the first one hundred cases with a special leather patch numbered 1/100, 2/100, 3/100, etc. and matched them with limited signed and numbered prints of that piece of grandfather art, 1/100, 2/100, etc. I also filled out an official certificate of authenticity and included it with each piece of signed artwork that came with the case. Those first 100 numbered cases sometimes sold out in a matter of seconds.

We then did different videos with the cases a "How It's Made" video that was filmed at the factory; a "Signing of the Artwork" video to reveal the name and design; a descriptive video of it somewhere cool, like Bosnia, Dubrovnik or Montenegro; and then a "What Fits" video to show the relative size of the case. It was a time intensive process, but the end result was really cool.

Art is something we create using a blend of natural skill and learned talent that gives people joy. The theme behind the Grandfather Collection campaign was art. We create functional art through our bags, and we created painted art to go with them, and we filmed everything artfully. And all of it brought people joy. It was a lot of work and our community enjoyed it.

LIFE AND DEATH BY A THOUSAND CUTS

In April of 2022, the lease was up on our huge concrete shoebox warehouse prison, so we moved to a small warehouse 15 minutes away, which was just 2 miles down the road from our home in Azle, Texas. People who know Azle laugh and say, "You moved to Azle!? Why Azle? There's nothing in Azle."

I'm not a mathematician, but I quickly did the numbers in my head and thought, *Let's see, they want to raise our rent to $28,000 per month. We can get a place in Azle for $13,000 per month. Why pay an extra $15,000 per month for rent in Fort Worth when 99 percent of our business is online anyways?* There certainly wasn't enough walk in traffic to justify paying the extra money, so we cut our costs and moved from Fort Worth to Azle.

The bigger plan was to open up the coolest headquarters in the whole world on the land Suzette and I had originally purchased to build our home on. By the way, I didn't say the *biggest* or *most expensive* headquarters in the whole world, just the *coolest*. We were cutting costs, after all.

In the meantime, I moved my really cool office into the showroom of the new, smaller warehouse and used it as a beautiful display there since I can work from my office and visit with customers who come into the showroom. We now lowered our cost of rent, but we still didn't know how much our bags cost and something was seriously wrong at the factory again. Pedro swore everything was fine and that we were profitable at the factory, but his numbers were ridiculously off. So, we started cutting costs there.

A year earlier, we had hired a successful and likable bulldog of a man named Jason Scoggins, as our COO, but as we were moving, he told me we didn't need him and that I should let him and several others go to lower costs. He said that's what he would do if it were his own business. In the end, we let about 7 people go in the US with their high salaries, and never replaced them since things were still flowing smoothly if not *more* smoothly than before. At that time, Suzette's sister, Tina, stepped up and shocked us all. I think she got struck by lightning, because while she had done good, solid work before, now she *majorly* stepped up, playing a strong leadership role keeping projects and IT on track.

And then we hired a consultant, Alex Ravikovich, to help us work on the factory. I told him we needed the factory to be profitable, our manufacturing prices to be competitive and to have accurate numbers. He said he could deliver. Alex had worked doing product development and overseeing factories around the world for Ralph Lauren for 11 years, and then worked for other big brands for another 6 years. After visiting our factory, he noticed something was seriously wrong too. Part of it, he said, was they were way overstaffed. I had been telling Pedro that same thing for 18 months, but he always had some sort of excuse why not to let anyone go.

By June of 2022, we decided to do another outside audit and submitted all of our books to a big accounting firm that specialized in Mexican businesses. They came back and told us that something was majorly wrong and the numbers just didn't add up. They suggested that instead of digging in and trying to find out the details, we should just fire whoever was in charge, later today, and start over. Alex and I immediately made charts of responsibilities and started firing people in the offices left and right, including Pedro. Altogether that year, we cut the cost of 62 full time salaried employees and went from 220 to 160 employees in a matter of months. The result? The factory didn't skip a beat. In fact, it became more efficient and we were adding so much money to the bottom line, we couldn't believe it.

FIFTEEN

Walking with Kings

In June of 2022, Suzette comes up to me and says, "You have to see this." She shows me a video of some friends of ours, the Bonnemas, walking on a path through trees while holding the tails of the wild lions walking in front of them. *What?* It turned out that Jacob Bonnema's son, Austin, and daughter-in-law, Tate, lived in Zambia, and a place, close by, where these ceremonial lions dwelled. They're not tame, but under certain circumstances, you can walk with them. They said now and then they attack someone, but not all that often, and their victims never die.

And then she showed me another video of them walking alongside rhinos out in the wilderness not further than 20 feet away. My mouth gaped wide open. We were in awe. I knew I must do this as well.

But I didn't know how soon until a few weeks later Austin informed us about the King of Kings conference. Overland Missions, the group Austin and Tate worked with, was hosting the largest gathering of African royalty in the history of the continent that October. The Forum of African Traditional Authorities (FATA) gathered from time to time, but always on a much smaller scale until now.

After the business side of the FATA meetings was to finish, they would continue the conference with other speakers, like the Grand Chief of the Cree Nation, who represents all Indian tribes in Canada at the United Nations, as well as other speakers and famous African musicians. Together, they were going to learn about The King of Kings.

Austin was told he could invite one person only, but he had a lot of friends and supporters to choose from and couldn't decide who it should be. So, he started praying and while he was praying, his phone dinged with a notification. He opened his eyes to see that a group chat had started with "Dave Munson and 3 Others" on his screen. He took it as an obvious sign to invite me.

Austin asked permission and they said Suzette could come in too, but Sela and Cross would have to stay at the hotel. We then told them we were bringing a photographer and videographer with us to walk with the lions, and the Overland leaders said they could really use their help at the King of Kings event. We agreed they could use them, but we needed Sela and Cross to assist them, because we didn't have anyone to stay with them at the hotel. In the end, our whole family and our 2 media people were allowed to come to the King of Kings conference.

Walking with lions and rhinos was enough to get us to Zambia one day, but add walking with kings to that list, and we had our plane tickets the next day.

THE WORK OF KINGS

Presidents are a relatively new thing in Africa. A few hundred years ago, the Europeans divvied up Africa by drawing country lines on a map of the continent, to make political borders for themselves to rule. In the 1960s and '70s, they gave Africans back their freedom and set up a political system of presidents and prime ministers to be elected by the people. Those politicians handle issues of import and export, taxes, education, the military, roads and so on.

Kings, on the other hand, have always been born into their position and have ruled the people of Africa for a thousand years, and they are responsible for judging all issues pertaining to their people and land. Since kings rule over people groups, not countries, their kingdom may extend into a neighboring country or two, and some countries have multiple kings. Some kings are worth billions of dollars, while others are very poor. But either way, their people generally love and respect them.

Philip Smethurst is the South African who founded Overland Missions, and he learned early on, if you want to serve the people, it is best to connect with the king and his chiefs rather than with politicians. Kings are so influential that, in some places, a person cannot even run for president without getting the nod from the king. So, to show the king or chief respect by asking his permission to work with his people goes a million miles.

But what Overland found is, as go the kings and chiefs, so go their people. The religion of a lot of the royalty is *animism*, where they worship their ancestors and the gods of trees, rivers, sun, clouds and more. And it often comes with a lot of witchcraft mixed in. When a new chief comes to his throne, he may sleep on the grave of the former chief for a week to get his power or drink the blood of the old chief from his skull. The local witch doctor is very important, as he casts spells and keeps the spirits of the ancestors happy. I don't understand it all, but I believe it is very dark and evil with a lot of demonic manifestation and possession going on. On the flipside, they see a lot of impossible things happen too. They experience so much of the supernatural, I've heard it said there are no atheists in Africa.

Overland Missions developed a great strategy. They tell the kings and their chiefs, "Many supreme rulers in the Bible had a man of God by their side: Pharoah had Joseph, Nebuchadnezzar had Daniel and David had Nathan. So, why don't you choose a local man of God, that you trust, to be trained by Overland to become your personal chaplain." They put Austin and Tate Bonnema, the ones who invited us to the King of Kings conference, in charge of the entire program

After the training, that chaplain begins to read the Bible to the chief, pray for him and his family and became a general trusted advisor. A lot of times, the chaplain becomes so trusted that when the chief travels, he leaves his chaplain in charge. The chiefs quickly learn of the great love of this new heavenly king and see the power of God actively working in the lives of their people, and so give their lives over to God too.

And since the chaplain has the authority of the chief, he is open to train and mentor the other local pastors, who likely have no biblical training themselves. A lot of times, the local pastors even mix animism and witchcraft into their Christian teachings on Sunday morning. Austin and Tate Bonnema, through Tribal Chaplaincy, are doing amazing work and Saddleback Leather is strongly behind them.

SERVANT OF THE KINGS

Upon arriving in Zambia, the Overland staff gave us the ground rules and etiquette for how to address and engage the 374 kings, queens, emperors, sultans, sheiks and chiefs in the country. If they were a king, queen, emperor or sultan, then it was His or Her Royal Majesty (HRM) or just His Majesty. If they were a prince, princess or a chief, we addressed them as His or Her Royal Highness (HRH). No selfies were allowed unless the royalty wanted one too, which they often did.

My role was to serve and drive the Zulu delegation wherever they needed to go. The new king could not come for the week, because his coronation was just a few weeks away, but he sent his Zulu warrior bodyguard to accompany and protect his friend, King Buki of Congo. He also sent his brother, Prince Andile, and then Prince Zolani, the senior parliament member of South Africa and president of the

Institute of African Royalty. Zolani was Nelson Mandela's poet laureate and the one who publicly introduced him to the world as president. Turns out, Zolani and I were born just 2 days apart from each other. I like that guy.

The first day of the event was a little awkward for everybody, since most of the royalty were not used to eating in front of others or even serving themselves at a buffet. One of the kings was indignant and angrily said to my son, "This is not right. A king should not wait in a line to eat food."

We weren't exactly sure how to act or approach them. Do we shake their hands? What are they comfortable talking about? Turns out, a lot of them don't have many friends, or at least they don't know who their true friends are because everyone either is required to be really nice to them or wants something from them. But we were just really nice and kind people who were interested in them and wanted to serve them, no strings attached.

Getting back from the airport with them, we started delivering room service meals to their rooms, since many of them were hungry from traveling. When I got to room 330, the door opened and I said, "Hello, Your Royal Majesty. How are you doing?"

The queen said, "Awful! I just realized I forgot all of my jewelry at my palace. What is a queen without her jewelry?"

I smiled and said, "Oh, don't you worry for a second, Your Majesty. You're talking to the right guy. My wife is here and she loves jewelry and will hook you up. Wait here and I'll send her right over." The queen was so happy.

So, I texted Suzette, but she didn't respond for an hour and a half. Turns out, she and the kids were pulled into a room by a different queen who just wanted to talk. Suzette asked her how her people greeted her on the street, and she said it was with their cheeks to the ground. They said she was very interesting to listen to, and they quickly became friends. In fact, Her Royal Majesty came to stay with us for a week in Texas last summer. Eventually, Suzette was able to help my queen with her jewelry issue.

The conference started with 3 days in Lusaka, the capital city of Zambia, and then continued for another 3 days in Livingston. We ate all of our meals with various kings, queens and emperors and naturally laughed and hugged and had a good time. Cross looked so handsome in his suit and Sela looked poised and stunning in her dresses. Since there were no other kids there, every visitor assumed they were royalty too.

I thought it was so funny to see a bunch of military personnel, assigned to security, gathered around Cross, asking him, " Where are you from?"

He proudly said, "I'm from Texas!" and immediately one of them said, "Oh, the Prince of Texas! Can we get photo? All of us?" So they started elbowing each other and jockeying for position to stand next to my 13 year old son, Cross Munson, "The Prince of Texas."

Each of us connected in such fun ways with the royalty. The king of Uganda and the prince of the Zulus both gave Cross noogies almost every time they saw him. Sela went up to the king from Niger and asked him, in French, if she could get a photo with him, and he went crazy. He *loved* that she tried to speak French. I asked, "If we were to visit Niger one day, is there a place where Sela and Cross could study French?"

He thought for a minute, and said, "They will learn French in my palace. You come to stay for one month with me and my family, and everyone will only speak French to them the whole time. Then they will learn French." Turns out, he came to visit us for 10 days in Texas and we had such a blast. He is a devout Muslim and still is, but we had GREAT conversations every day, throughout the day, about the commonalities and differences of our faiths. I learned so much and realized that the people of Niger are blessed to have a compassionate king like him who loves his people.

The kings from Egypt, Angola, Cameroon, Somalia, Congo, Ghana, Ethiopia, South Africa and other countries all invited us to come visit their kingdoms, because we had become friends. A couple of them said missionaries were not welcome, but since I was just a business owner, we could come anytime. By the end of the King of Kings conference, 38 kings asked to have the Tribal Chaplaincy program in their kingdoms, but Austin and Tate just don't have that much funding nor missionaries to train the chaplains to do it yet.

Another king and I have met up several times in London and in Rwanda to work on the vision for his kingdom. I can't mention his name because he comes from a very dangerous country and they wouldn't like it if they knew we were friends, but he's also a good man.

WALKING WITH LIONS

After the kings left, we hurried on over to where the ceremonial lions were. They warned us that walking with them would come with some risk. Some of the lions do attack from time to time, but no one has ever died. They gave us a stick, though, and said if they turn to bite us, then all we had to do was stick the stick in their mouths and we would be fine. I don't want to know how they learned this, but they did say they learned they can't let them be around children at all, because they show no mercy and go straight in for the kill everytime. Since Cross was only 13, he couldn't go, but since Sela was 15 she could.

I told Suzette, "If we let her go, we're going to hear the whole 'bad parent' thing forever, right?"

She agreed, but we all 3 agreed it was worth it. Sela walked with the lions for about 15 minutes and posted the video to her Instagram account when we got home. You should have heard her friends and co-workers at Chick-fil-A go wild about it. It's not like she was walking a tightrope over a pit of hungry crocodiles or anything. The worst thing that would probably happen was she would get a cool scar and a great story out of it.

Just after that trip, Sela was at work and one of her co-workers asked her, "So, where are you going next? Let me guess, you're going to go hang out with some kings or something?"

Since Sela hadn't told anyone about knowing or even hanging out with all of the kings, she gave him a bewildered look and responded, "How did you know about the kings?" He looked at her with his eyes wide and said, "What? Are you serious? I was just kidding." Sela told him that she did know some kings and even admitted that one king insists she call him "Uncle." When that same king was visiting us in Texas, with his big headdress and royal garb, he came into Chick-fil-A to say hi to her while she was working. You should have seen everyone stare.

SURPRISED IN LONDON

In November of 2022, Suzette somehow stumbled onto $189 round trip tickets to London for us to spend Christmas there and it was too good of a deal to pass up. We had always spent Christmas Day with either her family or mine, but Christmas 2022 was going to be different. We arrived in London and went to see a few of the 500 cool things there are to see and experience and then spent Christmas Day with a two foot tall plastic Christmas tree in our hotel room. It was kind of weird, and then Suzette and the kids got sick for a couple of days. That's when I decided to wander the city and scope out the competition.

I started on Bond Street, which is generally where the Who's Who of the fashion world has a store. The street was lined with Rolls Royces, Ferraris, Aston Martins and other exotic cars. It was fancy. Some of the stores even required an appointment to shop there. Louis Vuitton, Gucci, Hèrmes, Fendi, Prada, you name it, they were all there. And then I kept walking all around London.

Louis Vuitton had some good looking, high quality trunks, suitcases and smaller cases, but there was very little for sale anywhere else that I liked. This was particularly true of briefcases and duffle bags. They all seemed either too sterile and boring or too hip-hoppy exciting. Nothing inspired me.

I came to the conclusion, after browsing pretty much all of the competition in town, that we didn't have any competition in town . . . for people who shared my same tastes and personal style. To me, everything I saw in the most famous stores in the world was the same bag but with a different handle. They seemed to be all following the same trends and were boring to me. There was nothing inspiring or outstandingly beautiful. I felt that we could confidently open a store on Bond Street and thrive. We're not going to do that, but we could hold our own with the big boys. And this was confirmed a few months later.

DID SOMEONE SAY ROLLS ROYCE?

In early 2023, I received an email from St. James's House, a publisher in London, asking if they could put Saddleback Leather in their coffee table book, *Strive for Perfection*, that they were printing for Rolls Royce and the Rolls Royce and Bentley Enthusiast Club. Rolls Royce said we were a great fit for the book.

The book would go to all 11,000 of the Rolls Royce and Bentley Enthusiast Club members and each of the dealerships worldwide. Since it is hard to fill 350 to 400 pages with just pictures and text about Rolls Royces without it becoming boring, they wanted to fill in the book with companies who expressed the same passion for beautiful design and excessive quality as Rolls Royce.

I would have been shocked that a company with the prestige of Rolls Royce had invited us into this if I wouldn't have browsed the most famous stores in the world in London a few months earlier. I hadn't realized what Saddleback Leather had become over the years because I was just so used to it all.

WHAT BAG WOULD JAMES BOND CARRY?

At the Rolls Royce book launch party, I saw a dapper, well dressed gentleman in his mid-thirties walk by. He was wearing a very nice suit with nice shoes, but something was off. He was carrying a cheap and dumpy "My first big boy job" briefcase. That's when I realized he obviously borrowed the suit.

We sell *a lot* of bags for men who wear suits and uniforms in formal settings. One lawyer sent in a picture of himself with his briefcase standing on the steps of the Supreme Court just after he finished up a case there. Another lawyer told me that one time when he was in court, the judge asked him to approach the bench once the trial was over. He was nervous because he thought he was going to get his butt chewed out, but the judge just asked, "Hey, where did you get that bag?"

But now and then, a cleaner, more refined briefcase is in order. Customers have told me over the years that they *love* their Saddleback briefcases, but when they are going into a board meeting, they temporarily move over their stuff to a boring nondescript black bag because of the situation.

I designed my first Saddleback bag with the question, "What would Indiana Jones carry?" He was a professor and an archeologist, so he would carry a professional looking classic briefcase that would develop a patina and get broken in over time. The question I had to answer for more formal and refined settings was, "What would James Bond carry? He would carry a distinguished and refined something, yet stout and cool too." I've been designing for a tough James Bond that bleeds. Not the Timothy Dalton kind of James Bond, but the Daniel Craig version.

And that's the collection of bags I've been working on since 2011 but was struggling to get the exact look, finer details and timeless characteristics just right. Seeing the hundreds of boring bags around London that just didn't look right, along with the dozens of cool antique bags with details that did, was the key that opened the door of my design mind to understand what the James Bond-esque Collection required.

Walking the shops of London again with my marketing team after the Rolls Royce event, it became more than crystal clear to all of us that there was a gaping hole in the market for people who needed a cleaner, more refined bag to carry that was stout and cool and with plenty of naturalness.

THE HACKETT EFFECT

Over the years, my friend Steve Hackett had helped us significantly to think about the most important things in our business. In 2022, Steve retired from running the $12 billion business, and he and his wife, Cathy, were thoroughly taking advantage of their free time. But in March of 2023, he asked me about our business and how it was going. I told him it was going sort of okay, but asked if he would be willing to share more of his wisdom with us to help us with the factory. I told him we had some really big things going on, but our factory needed some concentrated tender loving care.

Steve graciously agreed and started working on not just the factory but our whole business right away. For the last many years, he had been in charge of evaluating the underperforming and struggling businesses that his company had acquired, then teaching them the basics and turning them around. He said all businesses struggle with the same things, and he always helped the leadership teams in those companies to see the business in the same basic way.

What and now he explained to them and trained them to do is exactly what he has been doing with us. He said, *"You're a successful leader if you lead your team to success at the bottom line and the way you do that is by running the business by the numbers."* I had heard these things a million times, but I never really understood practically and simply how to do it. Here is how Steve explained it to me that finally got through my thick skull. He started with what the bottom line was.

How many leadership books have you read, about inspirational, great communicators and innovative problem solving leaders who lead their people to defeat or no profit? None. They don't write books about people like that. But, if someone is a mean person, not a good communicator and fires anyone who questions them but still drives the team to success at the bottom line, then they are generally considered a great leader and someone writes a book about them. You have to lead your team to success at the bottom line, whatever that bottom line is.

Whether you lead at a church, a child sponsorship organization, a battered women's shelter, a restaurant, a factory, a retail business or it's just for your personal life, you need to understand, at a super basic level, what success looks like in what you do.

Every for-profit business regularly looks at what's called a profit and loss statement (P&L) to see how how much money they made or lost that month or year. And it's always laid out in 3 sections like this:

On the top line is the total of all the money that was deposited into the bank, either called "total sales" or "total revenue." Below that line is a list of all the costs or expenses it took to run the business and get the revenue number that is on the top line. These costs include salaries and benefits, materials or product, shipping, software, office supplies, marketing spend, rent, utilities, travel, coffee and all of the other expenses of the business.

They get that bottom line number by taking the top line of total of revenue and subtracting from it all of the costs that it takes to get all of those sales. *Sales minus Costs = Profit*. Say that 10 times slowly. This is super important. The bottom line tells us how much money we profited or how much money we lost at the end of the month or year.

In a regular for-profit business, it's only the profit on the bottom line that the success of the leader is judged by. Nothing else matters other than the bottom line. If the leader was a dear and loved man who was a fun and charismatic leader under whom everyone enjoyed their work, he would be fired at the end of the year if he did not lead his team to success at the bottom line. If you don't make money in a business, it's called a *hobby*.

This was a tough principle to get fully lodged into my brain. If you have a business, the bottom line is not to have a lot of activity and sell a bunch of stuff. It's not to give people jobs or pack out the auditorium or to be a fun cure for boredom. It's to walk away with money in the bank at the end of the year. What you do with the profit is a totally different matter. I don't care if you give it all to the poor, give monster bonuses to employees, build an orphanage or buy a chalet in France, that's up to you. But the goal of a leader is to drive the team to make sure there's money in the bank at the end of the year.

The bottom line is not always measured in money. For a battered women's shelter, it's not about how many women were helped, but about how many women no longer get into bad relationships with horrible men. For a basketball team, it's not about how many passes were made or shots were taken, the bottom line is did you score more points than the opponent. For the pastor of a church, it's not about how many people ended their lives fat and happy, but about how many people came to believe in God and truly know Him.

Any ethical counselor or consultant will have the same bottom line as a good doctor: to help or train you how to have a healthy marriage, life, body or business, and to do it in as short of a time as possible. Their goal should not be to have you as a regular client or patient for the next 10 years. If they are skillful, you'll never need to see them again.

We had heard that our marriage counselor, Mark Foster, at Restoration in Fort Worth is the best in town and we believe it. He listened to our gripes and irritations and then coached us for 5 or 6 one hour sessions, and that helped our marriage be better. It was incredible. He was successful at the bottom line. By the way, every couple should go to marriage counseling. Who doesn't want to help their spouse feel more loved and cherished and have a better marriage? It's like preventative maintenance for your car.

For Dave Munson, when I get to Heaven and I'm judged on the bottom line, I believe my bottom line will not be about the number of quality bags I designed and sold, though God created us to do excellent work and that pleases Him. It won't be about how nice I was to people or about how much I talked about God. Instead, my bottom line will be how obedient I was to do what God asked me to do. He commands us to love Him and to love our neighbor as we love our own self. That's the bottom line for my life.

More specifically, what does that look like? God told me to go tell people the good message (aka the gospel) about how He sent Jesus to die on the cross to pay for our sins so we wouldn't have to pay for them, then He was buried and after 3 days He was raised from the dead. If you believe that good message in your heart, then you're a believer. That's the good message and, the bottom line is, God commanded all of His followers to tell people that good news. And I just told it to you.

And I also believe I will get rewards in Heaven for being a witness for Him, because He said I will. I believe that whatever God says is true. I put my faith in God. I trust Him. And if God asks me why I should be able to come into Heaven, I will tell him, "God, I believed You when You told me Your son paid for all of my sin, was buried and rose again. That's all I got."

RUNNING A BUSINESS BY THE NUMBERS

While Steve's emphasis on running the business by the numbers seemed like what Saddleback needed, I still was not sure what exactly that meant. So, Steve told me about this man named Vilfredo Pareto (1848-1923). Pareto was an Italian economist who noticed that about 80 percent of the wealth in Italy belonged to about 20 percent of the people. He then saw that about 80 percent of a company's sales came from about 20 percent of its customers and products; 80 percent of all crimes were committed by 20 percent of all criminals; and 80 percent of all land belonged to about 20 percent of the population. It's the 80/20 Rule, or the Pareto Principle.

Pareto said that 80 percent of output is the result of 20 percent of input. In other words, 20 percent of the tasks on your to-do list will account for 80 percent of your results. Reread the last 2 sentences 3 times slowly and let it soak in.

Instead of sorting your 10 to-dos by their deadlines, sort them in order of how big of an impact they will be to whatever your bottom line is. Then focus all of your, or your team's, time and money on accomplishing the 2 or 3 tasks that most impact your bottom line. That's called "Pareto sorting," and it's how you run a business by the numbers.

Here is how Steve explained it. Let's say they acquire a business with $100 million of total annual sales and found that all of the costs it took to sell that much was $90 million. You end up with $10 million in profit (or 10 percent) at the end of the year. You now have 2 options to get more profit: You can either raise your sales and keep the costs the same or lower your costs and keep the sales the same. Removing costs is always the easiest and most immediate impact to the bottom line.

So let's "Pareto sort" all of the cost categories in this $100 million business, from biggest to smallest, or, in other words, in order of which ones will make the biggest difference to the bottom line:

1. $50 million for payroll and related expenses
2. $25 million for materials
3. $10 million for shipping

4. $5 million for software
5. $4 million for rent
6. $3 million for packaging
7. $2 million for training
8. $1 million for office supplies and miscellaneous expenses

Let's say you worked hard and cut costs on #4 through #8 on the list by 10 percent. You start recycling office paper, buy cheaper coffee for the office, install light timers in the bathrooms, reduce the size of your boxes, move to a place for cheaper rent, stop paying for software you rarely use and bingo! you saved $1.5 million, which is added to the profit or bottom line. That is 1.5 percent more profit. Now you're at 11.5 percent profit in total on the bottom line.

But what if, instead, you spent time cutting costs from #1, #2 and #3 on the list by 10 percent? You spend time negotiating lower prices for raw materials by 5 percent and figure out how to get 5 percent more out of the raw materials by cutting better. That gives you $2.5 million (2.5 percent) more profit. Then you look at shipping and negotiate rates and consolidate shipments and cut 10 percent there, which is $1 million (1 percent) more profit. Then you look at your bloated payroll expenses and cut 10 percent there for $5 million (5 percent) more profit. Bingo! That adds up $8.5 million straight to the bottom line for profit. Now you're at 18.5 percent profitability.

So, according to Steve's model, you should spend all of your time trimming the fat off the top 3 biggest costs, *period*. Don't even look at #4 until you reduce #1, #2 and #3 as much as possible. Remember, Pareto said that 80 percent of output is the result of 20 percent of input. In other words, 20 percent of the tasks on your to-do list will account for 80 percent of your results.

Steve helped us apply these principles to Saddleback. We started by "Pareto sorting" our biggest to littlest costs, and it was clear what we needed to do next. We had just made major payroll cuts in the

US and at the factory in Mexico, but there were more we still needed to cut. Then I negotiated with the tanneries to get the price down about 3 percent and talked with our head of cutting, Isabel, to figure out how the cutters could cut the leather better. It was a lot of work, but they started getting about 7 percent better yield out of each hide without lowering the quality of the product. Our custom 316 stainless steel hardware is *very* expensive, so I talked with the owner of the hardware company, and he said that if we ordered more hardware in advance, then it would make it cheaper for him on the raw materials side and he could pass the savings on to us.

Now that we'd significantly lowered costs in the top 2 cost areas, payroll and materials, we "Pareto sorted" our marketing ideas. We sorted them by which efforts would be the most impactful to immediately increase sales without increasing costs. We had 2 marketing category options to Pareto sort:

1. To get more people to come to the website to buy something.
2. To get more of the people who were already coming to the site to buy something.

We decided Option 2 takes way less money and effort and will immediately grow sales. Next we "Pareto sorted" all of the most common questions that customer service received from people and sorted those and focused on answering those on the product details pages so it would be easier for people to make a decision and pull the trigger.

The most important questions customers had boiled down to 2 categories: *Which one should I get?* and *Is this leather bag really worth it?*

We determined the main reason people weren't buying was because they couldn't figure out which one they should get. So, instead of making funny brand videos about how tough the bags are, we separated the briefcases into three categories: Large, Standard and

Minimalist. Then, we described them: Do you like the plain traditional flap look, the pocketed look or the hinged opening? For the duffles, we separated the 8 duffle bags into Check Ins or Carry Ons. In the carry ons, we asked, Do you want a bag for 2 to 3 days or one for 3 to 5 days?

We put descriptive words and measurements on pictures and showed pictures of the bags on different sized people. And to decide which products to do all of this to, we "Pareto sorted" the designs by most popular and then that design by most popular color.

You can also "Pareto sort" your restaurant, ministry, home or basketball team. Here's your homework: Think through which 2 or 3 things on your to-do list will make the biggest difference in achieving your bottom line. Whether the bottom line is the most profit, the most souls in Heaven or the most lives changed, focus your attention on those 2 or 3 things that will have the biggest impact on you achieving your bottom line. And remember what Pareto discovered: 80 percent of output is the result of 20 percent of input.

CONCLUSION
Saddleback Leather Today

So, what's going on now in 2025? Well, the announcement video Toyota released with the truck was very honoring and full of Saddleback Leather praise and admiration. They did us right. Each of the numbered Limited Edition Tundras (1 of 1,500, 2 of 1,500 etc.) came with a special Saddleback Leather Duffle Bag and other car accessories that we made with the same thick automotive leather. It was so cool.

I received my own truck in April of 2024 and it felt so amazing to finally sit in it. It is a constant reminder that God does what He wants, when He wants, and He uses us sometimes too. The Saddleback Leather Edition Toyota Tundra name was changed to the 1794 Limited Edition Toyota Tundra because a copyright issue with an aftermarket carseat company who sold "Saddleback leather carseat covers." If Toyota launched the Saddleback Leather Tundra, they would be sued within the hour.

We finally broke ground on the coolest headquarters in the whole world and will be moving in, in just a few months. There will be a lot of work to do to make it the coolest, but first things first, let's move in. We started selling the highest quality boots that we could make and other styles are on the way. The only way we could get the level we did was for them to be made in Italy. Now I have to travel back and forth to Italy. And, we are finally releasing the refined Silverback Collection made with an Italian leather and lined in fine and tough goatskin, in the fall of 2025, which has been 14 years in the making.

Well that's about all there is to the Saddleback Story so far. Thanks for hearing me out. I hope this book helped you to think differently about life and business and God, and hopefully your life will be a little better than it was before you read this book. I hope it encouraged you to jump in and try what has been on your heart to do for a while. I have to say that just starting and figuring all of the boring stuff later has worked for me and it'll work for you too. I just know it.

As you know by now, God used both the good and the bad to shape the Saddleback Story, and He shaped and molded me and my pride at the same time. Despite all the mistakes and wrong turns, I like how I turned out, but especially I like what my company became. I wouldn't trade any of it for anything (except for maybe the time in Belize, when my friend Javier Prado lanced my gums with a Leatherman to try to relieve the pressure from my bad abscessed tooth. That was dumb and it didn't even help the pain. And I ended up losing that tooth anyways. But other than not having dental insurance, if I could go back in time for a re-do, I wouldn't change a thing.)

I am curious to see what the future holds, but we'll just keep on trying to design beautiful things that are made with quality. We've had some fun and exciting times and if all of this happened in 21 years, I can only imagine the stories we'll have after the next 21 years. I've got a feeling that the best is yet to come.

ACKNOWLEDGMENTS

To God. Your patience with me and how You don't stop working on me is amazing. You placed me in my family, shaped my tastes, gave me gifts and have included me in what You're doing. Thank You.

To my wife, Suzette. Your compassionate and others focused heart has pulled us into deep and meaningful relationships around the world. I don't know how you do it so consistently, but I'm so glad you do. Thank you.

To my mom, Carol. You prayed throughout the day, every day, to move God's hand to keep us alive and in business, and you gave us an example of selflessness like I have never seen in my life. Thank you. I miss you, Mom.

To my dad, Herb. You made spending time with all of us kids a priority, which helped me to understand my worth in this world. You gave me an excellent example of how to be a husband and father and how to just jump in and figure out the rest later. I also love how you wisely explained deep spiritual truths over and over again in simple ways that I could understand. What a GREAT father you are. Thank you.

To Mickey, the greatest editor in the industry. The way you took this book from almost 600 pages to what it is today and made it flow so perfectly is nothing short of miraculous. Thank you.

Last, but not least, to our faithful Saddleback Leather customers. You have supported us all these years, even during COVID when you didn't need what we had to offer. You have loved us and a lot of people around the world by doing what you do. Thank you.